On the Record

An Insider's Guide to Journalism

D0393660

On the Record
An Insider's Guide to Journalism

Tom Wicker

Bedford/St. Martin's
Boston ♦ New York

For Bedford/St. Martin's

Communication Editor: Jennifer Bartlett
Developmental Editor: Michael Bagnulo
Senior Production Editor: Michael Weber
Senior Production Supervisor: Joe Ford
Marketing Manager: Richard Cadman
Art Direction and Cover Design: Lucy Krikorian
Composition: Stratford Publishing Services
Printing and Binding: Haddon Craftsmen, Inc., an R. R. Donnelley & Sons Company

President: Charles H. Christensen
Editorial Director: Joan E. Feinberg
Editor in Chief: Nancy Perry
Publisher for History and Communication: Patricia Rossi
Director of Marketing: Karen R. Melton
Director of Editing, Design, and Production: Marcia Cohen
Managing Editor: Erica T. Appel

Library of Congress Control Number: 2001087207

Manufactured in the United States of America.

7 6 5 4 3 2
f e d c b a

For information, write: Bedford/St. Martin's, 75 Arlington Street,
Boston, MA 02116   (617-399-4000)

ISBN: 0-312-25844-5

Preface

I once thought of naming this book *Lost in Cyberspace,* and for good reason.

The old-fashioned craft of journalism, after all, seemed out of place in the astounding modern world of digital wizardry, global communications, the World Wide Web, modems, e-mail, chips, bauds, dot-com addresses, electronically contrived backgrounds, million-dollar IPOs for techno-firms yet to earn a dollar, nerds too young to vote and too rich to care. In such a new-fashioned world, journalism seemed dated and deservedly so, an ill-reputed relic in an e-attic, on the shelf with rabbit-ear antennae and eight-track audio.

When AOL-Time Warner can and probably will open the world's biggest shopping mall, moreover, who cares about the barriers that once separated news and advertising? If CBS-TV can superimpose its logo on the General Motors building while the commercial-makers resurrect John Wayne, don't journalism's antique sins of unidentified sources and editorializing in the news mean about as much as or as little as the old Linotype keyboard's *etaoinshrdlu*? And since any clever hack can fill the Internet with gossip, propaganda, rumors and lies, what's the use of trained reporters and editors? In a universe moving inexorably into fakery — the virtual, the simulated, the hyped — who needs an old-world craft devoted, at its infrequent best, to merely reliable information, dispassionately presented?

The more the world was absorbed by and in media, the more life seemed to me to *become* media. My late mentor James Reston — the most enthusiastic and ingenious reporter I've known — used to contend that he and I were living in an "age of journalism," of real happenings more amazing than the fiction he thought I was foolish to want to write. But that was before Silicon Valley converted the same era to an "age of media," which is a vastly different concept from Reston's, with far greater potential for invention and fantasy than the most imaginative novel.

Already, in the United States, if an event can't be seen on television, it scarcely registers on the national nervous system; in effect, it hasn't really happened. In addition, prime-time and commercial heroes are now like our neighbors: "I'm not a doctor but I play one on TV." As virtual reality becomes *the* reality for most people, why would they believe in anything unrecorded, or not contrived, by media?

Although lately journalism has been swamped with breathless reports of electronic marvels and breathtaking mergers, journalism is or should be concerned with the un-virtual. In short, writers and editors should continue to tell us about the known victory, the acknowledged defeat, the inevitable follies and foibles, triumphs and tragedies of whatever humanity and world continue to exist outside the computer and the TV screen.

As I contemplated this book, it seemed to me mostly an act of faith to believe there would be such a world, however marginal. On the other hand, the Industrial Revolution didn't totally revolutionize life. So perhaps the Communications Revolution, though possibly even more sweeping, might not, after all, fundamentally alter human nature, what Faulkner called "the old truths of the human heart." And even in the twenty-first century, as in the last, humankind might continue to ask where it's been and how it got *here,* of all places. If so, though the "first draft of history" that journalism traditionally provided probably wouldn't furnish a fully adequate answer — it never had — honest and perceptive reporting still might record useful raw material for the later harsh revisions of scholarship.

If that were true, then maybe even in the primacy of media, journalism would continue to matter enough, to enough people, so that a few seriously intended news reports — print or broadcast or Internet or whatever — might survive. In that perhaps forlorn hope, I chose for my title *On the Record* because the record of events is what journalism tries inadequately to keep. Therefore, this primer on journalism may prove helpful: first, to those who still aspire to practice the craft; and second, to those who consider journalism a form of opening other people's mail and its practitioners on a level with grave-robbers.

It may confound these latter to learn, if they will, that most reporters are neither paparazzi chasing princesses on motorcycles nor gimlet-eyed inquisitors thrusting microphones into hapless faces while demanding, "How does it feel to be the president's mistress?" or "How does it feel to be the deceived wife"? And it may surprise neophyte journalists to learn, as they'll have to, that journalism is not a trade with clear and positive rules that one need only learn and follow.

In fact, every day a journalist is likely to be confronted with complex questions of procedure that can't be ducked but to which there's no undisputed answer. Despite its apologists, journalism is essentially a process without rules, except for vast abstractions like honor and integrity, which on any given occasion may be viewed differently by different people.

Despite common public and political accusations, however, reputable newspapers and broadcasters seldom commit the unforgivable sin of journalism: deliberately and knowingly propagating an untruth. But the harder question journalists often face is *What is the truth?* Or *What can I reasonably believe is the truth?* And sometimes they face an even more difficult problem: *What is responsible in this situation?* The answers to such questions can be obscure and debatable, and are not covered in any code of ethics or rule book — including this primer.

I often faced such choices and dealt with them by my (sometimes dim) lights. For that reason, many examples cited here date from what may now appear to some Americans as a "golden age" — the era of Kennedy, Johnson, even Nixon — but to others as prehistoric. Dates aside, however, these examples are intended to reflect *principles,* not hard-and-fast rules, that should be integral to journalism now as then, in the future as well as in the past, whether in print, on the air or downloaded.

What is news anyway? How important is it? How and how well does the press act, or try to act, as a watchdog for the public interest? What about the celebrated conflict between the individual's right to privacy and the public's right to know? Isn't the press supposed to be objective? And why isn't press freedom balanced with press responsibility? Why did all those unnamed people babbling on about Monica Lewinsky or Kenneth Starr have a place in the news? Or do they?

Principles can help to answer such questions — as this book tries to do — but the practical application of principles is likely to be in the eye of the beholder, not rigid or immutable. With or without principles, journalism is replete with the need for choice; decisions are necessarily made by fallible humans with no magic compass, only their conception of principle, to point the right way to go in any specific case. Choices made in such circumstances often will appear, to those who disagree, as dishonest or irresponsible. And the hard fact is that a journalist may well make a difficult decision wrongly, without sufficient information or reflection and perhaps self-indulgently. Or a journalist may go wrong even *after* every precaution has been taken, every consideration pondered, all principles consulted. Journalists are not truth machines, as no one is.

Error, then, is a hazard of journalism that can't be countered with a classroom course or an old-timer's lecture; that's why some historians have learned to take newspaper accounts of yesterday's events with a grain of salt. Still, journalists must do the best they can with what they know, or believe they know, in the time available, to satisfy the public's voracious appetite for information. In any fair judgment, it's remarkable how often in the past the public's need to know has been reasonably well served. And it still may be, even by different means, in the future.

Therefore, for a public that, if given the chance, might do away with freedom of the press, and for would-be journalists dazzled by the stardom of Peter Jennings or Tom Brokaw and reared on exotic tales of Woodward and Bernstein, *On the Record* will attempt to describe not only what the press does and thinks it's doing — not always the same thing — but why and under what limitations. It won't tell beginners precisely how best to satisfy the public's demand for information; probably nothing can do that. Nor, with the best of intent, is this book certain to persuade critics that journalism is not an irresponsible calling with an unslakable thirst for power and profit because sometimes, unfortunately, it is.

At best, however, those hard choices journalism inevitably poses have been made and will be made in keeping with the only real criteria journalists have: the honor and integrity that their craft and its mission demand, that their lives should have inculcated in them. To both public and practitioner, *On the Record* will insist on those guidelines. All others are sure to be disputed.

Tom Wicker

Contents

On the Record

An Insider's Guide to Journalism

CHAPTER 1

Choices

On Nov. 8, 1960, the fabled Kennedy-Nixon presidential election took place. One of the closest presidential elections in history, it was also the last in which more than 60 percent of Americans voted. Just after 9 p.m., the first edition of *The New York Times* hit the street, a headline blaring from page one:

KENNEDY ELECTED

That headline reflected not only the early returns from Eastern states but also the beliefs, in some instances the hopes, of the *Times* reporters around me.

A rookie in the newsroom, I had been assigned the relatively low-level job of reporting the various governors' elections being held around the nation that same day. Having finished fairly early, I had little to do but watch the bustling election-night activity in the huge newsroom that stretches between 43rd and 44th streets in Manhattan.

At about 1 a.m. on Nov. 9, Turner Catledge, the managing editor, conferred with his closest associates near the national news desk. Suddenly, he made a short, sharp uppercutting gesture with his clenched fist and then stalked off toward his corner office with a determined look on his face.

Or maybe it was more nearly a resigned look. Shortly thereafter, the *Times'* second edition rolled off the presses with another huge but quite different headline across the top of page one:

KENNEDY APPARENTLY ELECTED

I had witnessed a historic moment: The managing editor of what was then indisputably the most influential newspaper in the world had

1

recognized that the election returns beginning to creep in from the Midwest and the Rocky Mountain states were mostly benefiting the Republican candidate, Vice President Richard M. Nixon. Catledge's uppercut had signaled that *The New York Times* would, in newspaper jargon, "climb down" from its early, overconfident proclamation of victory for the Democrat, Senator John F. Kennedy of Massachusetts.

There was more to the moment than that, however. I did not know it then but I believe now that I had witnessed something like the exact moment when American newspapers began to rely on television, rather than the other way around. I had seen the emergence of media and technology as the dominating forces in journalism.

Turner Catledge and other editors had been watching the TV sets scattered around the *Times* newsroom. As the television reports followed the westward curve of the night's events, tallying the Nixon gains that had come too late for the *Times'* first edition, Catledge had had the courage to recognize the inevitable. Even if belatedly, he went along with the more current data on TV.

Catledge was not retracting a lie, however, when he directed the climb down from that first incautious *Times* headline. Instead, he was correcting a premature conclusion, one that was warranted perhaps by the "facts" — early returns — on which it had been based, even though they later turned out to be incomplete and misleading. Catledge's act was one of those tough decisions about which nothing said in journalism school offers much of a guide. No *rule* required the *Times* to call the election for Kennedy in its first edition; and no rule demanded that the managing editor change that call when later facts appeared. Rather, in both instances, fallible humans made judgments based on what they thought was the best information available. And even if Catledge had stood by that first headline, events ultimately would have justified it; Kennedy did finally win.

Any number of die-hard Nixon Republicans believe to this day, however, that the *Times'* first-edition headline was just another deliberate "liberal" attempt by the "Eastern internationalist press" to sway the electorate to the Left and in favor of the Democratic candidate. (After all, polls still were open in the West, and potential Nixon voters in those states might have been influenced to think that the election was all over, with "Kennedy elected.") Such Americans, remembering that first headline among other real or imagined offenses, are likely still to denounce the "liberal press," as Nixon himself did (on other grounds).

* * *

Before that election night — before that general period, anyway —
and for most of television's early history, on any major breaking-news
story, TV broadcasts tended to follow the lead of newspapers and the
wire services. Some TV news broadcasters of the time have since confessed that they occasionally even read from newspaper clippings. Walter Cronkite, heightening the drama of a drought in Kansas, once
burned a printed map of the area while cameras of WTOP-TV in Washington filmed the miniature blaze.

Cronkite and other early TV newscasters had several problems
vis-à-vis print journalism. First of all, *The New York Times* and other
printed journals had more highly developed organizations and communications facilities and more reporters scattered around the nation
and the world. And television, then as now, was heavily dependent on
film that was not easily obtained or transmitted. In addition, many of
the early television news broadcasters were former print or radio
reporters and were still somewhat contemptuous of the new medium.
They doubted that they or the TV screen could come up to the sophisticated level of more established journalism.

Imperceptibly but inexorably, however, television news services
grew and matured. By 1960, the three leading networks had a worldwide roster of correspondents who were better able to keep up with the
flow of news — and U.S. elections returns — than any newspaper, the
Times included. Nor did men like Cronkite or David Brinkley any
longer lack confidence in themselves or in television, if they ever had,
to get the job done.

Lured by higher salaries, greater opportunities, or both, numerous
print and radio journalists had begun to enlist with the new medium.
When I started covering the White House for the *Times* in mid-1961, I
replaced William H. Lawrence,[1] a veteran of domestic and foreign print
reporting who had jumped to ABC News (then headed by James
Hagerty, who had been President Dwight D. Eisenhower's press secretary). Lawrence was miffed that the *Times* had refused to let him go to
Europe to cover one of President Kennedy's early trips abroad (James
Reston already was there and could do the job); but ABC-TV was
happy to sign a prominent recruit from print journalism.

President Kennedy recognized and enhanced the potential of television news. He allowed his frequent news conferences to be televised

---

[1] He was known as "Political Bill" to distinguish him from another William Lawrence
on the *Times* staff, who was known as "Farmer Bill" because he covered agriculture.

"live" and located TV reporters and cameras in the most advantageous audience positions to record his wit and charisma. (I believe his popular news conferences were a major element in the near-canonization later accorded him.) It was during this time that network reporters (almost always males in those days) began to share the press pool aboard Kennedy's *Air Force One* with old-line newspaper types, not always to the latter's liking.

The men with cameras and sound equipment (an irreverent bunch indeed) who had crowded the White House press lobby in 1961 mostly represented the old movie-theater newsreels. But by Nov. 22, 1963, when Kennedy was murdered, the reels had virtually disappeared, replaced by the major TV network news operations.

During that memorable weekend of Kennedy's death, television stayed on the air for more than 70 hours, unbroken by commercials and accompanied by classical music. The TV networks not only reported the events of the assassination but also helped "hold the nation together," as others have noted. In the process, I believe, TV news became what it remains today — a sort of national nervous system on which something has to register before that something is generally believed to have happened. It's hard, even for old-timers, to remember now — and most Americans have never known — the era when television news was mostly a rehash of what had already appeared in the morning paper.

Just as Turner Catledge[2] made a difficult decision on election night 1960, he and *Times* publisher Orvil Dryfoos made an even more difficult journalistic decision several months later. It was one for which Catledge afterwards would be criticized to his face by the president of the United States himself.

On April 6, 1961 — not yet three months into the Kennedy administration — a *Times* reporter, Tad Szulc, filed a story about Cuban refugees being trained in Guatemala by the Central Intelligence Agency for an invasion of Fidel Castro's Cuba on April 18. This was a hot potato in more ways than one. Not only was a military operation affecting national security involved — a most serious matter at any time but especially then, with the Cold War at its height — and not only was Kennedy's "New Frontier" scarcely in office; but the *Times* was extraordinarily sensitive about its Cuba coverage because it fre-

---

[2] Gay Talese, a former *Times* reporter, once aptly wrote that Catledge's hand was in everything, his fingerprints on nothing.

quently had been accused of being "soft on Castro." (The charge arose
from stories about the Cuban revolution by Herbert Matthews, a first-
rate and long-experienced reporter whom even some *Times* editors
thought had become too involved with the Castro movement.)

Recognizing the volatility of the Szulc file, subordinate *Times* editors quickly eliminated the predicted invasion date before Catledge
even saw the story; their edited version said the invasion was merely
"imminent." When the managing editor did see the article, he quickly
told Dryfoos, who worried that by alerting Castro to the planned
attack, the story would support the "soft on Castro" charge against the
Times. Catledge and Dryfoos then called James Reston, the Washington bureau chief. After making some inquiries of high-level sources —
including CIA chief Allen Dulles! — Reston recommended that
Szulc's story not be published.[3]

Catledge, however, would not go that far. With the approval of Orvil
Dryfoos, he did eliminate the "imminent" reference and — though
Reston had not told him about calling Dulles — removed any mention
of the CIA, an agency for which too much reverence once existed
among too many journalists. More important, the managing editor
vetoed the original front-page layout, in which Szulc's story would have
occupied the prominent top right-hand position beneath a blaring four-
column headline. This was the major spot in any newspaper, but putting
the story in this location would have been especially startling in the staid
Times of that day. Catledge ordered the story moved to column four, still
at the top of page one but under a conservative, one-column headline —
a distinct move to downplay the story.

It can be and has been argued that once the invasion date and all
references to the CIA were eliminated, Szulc's story no longer merited
top play. That's a plausible explanation, but diminishing the prominence, to such an extent, of so momentous a story was still a challenging decision for any editor to make.

In his memoirs, Catledge himself cited a different line of reasoning. He said he acted on the fear that many lives would be lost in the
invasion and that the *Times* would be blamed for exposing the plan in
time for the Cubans to prepare their defenses.[4]

In fact, the invasion took place on April 17, 1961, a day earlier
than Szulc's original prediction. (The timing raises an interesting

---

[3] Many years later, Reston told me he regretted having done so.
[4] Turner Catledge, *My Life and the Times* (New York: Harper & Row, 1971).

after-the-fact question: Is a story that appears on April 7 correct in reporting that an invasion, which will take place on April 17, is "imminent"? Is ten days in the future "imminent"? Or does the word suggest, as it does to me, "right away," certainly in the next day or two?)

In any event, the story still was the last thing the *Times* wanted: a "red alert" to the Cubans. Unfortunately, however, the story was not sufficient warning for President Kennedy. The invasion at the infamous Bay of Pigs was easily repelled by the Cubans, 114 lives were lost, and a thousand invaders were captured. They, the plan itself, and the president's refusal to order U.S. air support became continuing political embarrassments for the Kennedy administration, and Allen Dulles was forced to resign.

In my view, Dulles' fate was richly deserved. He later told me that he had forced a reluctant Kennedy to approve the Bay of Pigs invasion by asking him, "Are you going to be less anti-Communist than Eisenhower?" Kennedy's predecessor, President Eisenhower, had authorized the formation of the Cuban force. Eisenhower liked to refer to Kennedy as "the young whippersnapper" and Kennedy could not afford for voters to believe that he fit this description, as Allen Dulles well knew.

Though the Bay of Pigs fiasco was rarely blamed on the *Times* story, Kennedy first called the story "indiscriminate and premature." Later, he actually said in a speech that publishers should ask of every news story: "Is it in the interest of national security?" A lot of Americans probably would agree with that rationale, dismissing any conflict with the First Amendment.

In a later meeting with a group of editors, however, the president said privately to Turner Catledge: "Maybe if you had printed more about the operation, you would have saved us from a colossal mistake." Still later, even more remarkably, the president told Orvil Dryfoos: "I wish you had run everything on Cuba . . . I'm just sorry you didn't tell it at the time."

These remarks speak volumes about the supposed sanctity of the government's conception of national security, and about press deference to that conception. Moreover, the decisions made on that long-ago April 6 illustrate clearly the point that many major journalistic choices cannot be made "by the book." All too often there simply is no book.

In the case of Szulc's story, editors and even the publisher disputed what to do. Reston wanted to protect national security. Dryfoos was worried about appearing soft on Castro. Catledge wrote later that he wanted to protect the newspaper from charges that it had caused death on the invasion beaches. No doubt all three shared some of the same fears. Even the secondary editors who were angry that the story was being downplayed for political reasons had scratched the actual invasion date.

My own judgment, and I believe that of history, is that the *Times* should have printed Szulc's story as it was written, letting the chips fall where they might. Maybe JFK was even correct that a "colossal mistake" then would have been avoided because a bold press would have acted independently. (Few presidents, though, on that or any grounds normally urge the press to print or broadcast stories they don't like.)

All of this is, of course, hindsight. I wasn't part of those deliberations on April 6, 1961, and even if I had been I would have been no more sure of what to do — what was *responsible* — than were Reston, Catledge and Dryfoos. They were in the midst of a classic journalistic dilemma: They held great power but could not be *certain* what to do with it. They did what they thought best, and though I believe they were wrong, I'm not sure I would have handled the situation differently — or better.

More than 10 years later, in another unprecedented dilemma but a vastly different context, the *Times* made up for whatever error might have been committed on the truncated Bay of Pigs story. So did James "Scotty" Reston. On his advice and that of others, the newspaper published on June 13, 1970, what was to become famous as the "Pentagon Papers." Then, despite furious opposition from the Nixon administration, the *Times* won vindication from the Supreme Court in a historic confirmation of press freedom.

Let's look first at the background of this journalistic decision. Turner Catledge had been succeeded as managing editor, first by E. C. Daniel and then by the incumbent, Abe Rosenthal. Orvil Dryfoos had died a shockingly early death, and Arthur O. Sulzberger had become publisher. Presidents Kennedy and Lyndon B. Johnson had come and gone, as presidents do. Richard Nixon was in the White House, and the Cold War was still going on. Castro's Cuba was as unpopular as ever, but the focus of public interest had shifted to the war in Vietnam.

By 1970 that war was at least five years old (dating from the formal entry of U.S. troops into combat in 1965) and was no longer known as "Johnson's War." It had become "Nixon's War." Public hostility to a seemingly endless and hopeless "bitch of a war on the other side of the world" (as LBJ privately called it) was intense; many of those who hated the war (including many who had originally supported it) hated the Nixon administration almost as much.

Nixon did not know, nor did virtually anyone else, that during the Johnson administration, as Secretary of Defense Robert McNamara began to lose faith in the Vietnam effort, he had ordered a history of U.S. involvement in Vietnam to be compiled, complete with memoranda, transcripts, and all the vital records of secret deliberations and decisions. One of those who had contributed material to this history, and who had read the rest of it, was Daniel Ellsberg, a youthful "defense intellectual" at the Rand Corporation think tank, which was often employed by the Defense Department.

I had met Ellsberg in Saigon on one of my reporting trips there in 1966; then, he had been a fire-eating former Marine lieutenant dedicated to winning a war he fervently believed in. By the time he contributed to McNamara's history, though, he (like many other Americans) was fervently opposed to what he had come to see as an immoral or unwinnable war, or both. In the belief that he might help extricate the United States from its floundering involvement in Southeast Asia, Ellsberg had started to wonder how he could put McNamara's secret history before the public.

I'm not sure when Ellsberg decided to let Neil Sheehan, then a *Times* Pentagon reporter, see the material. One day in 1968, however, he and Sheehan called on me in my office as the *Times* Washington bureau chief.

"You guys have been conned," Ellsberg told me right off.

According to Ellsberg, General William C. Westmoreland, the U.S. commander in Vietnam, and Ellsworth Bunker, the ambassador to the Saigon regime, had greatly exaggerated the extent of American successes in the war during their visit to Washington in the fall of 1967. Their rose-colored account nevertheless had been duly accepted by most of the press.

That wasn't all. "You should have seen what they *wanted* to tell you," Ellsberg continued.

In preparing for their visit to Washington, he said, Westmoreland and Bunker had cabled the Pentagon with the details of what they originally planned to say. Their claims were so inflated that even Pentagon officials saw at once they'd never be believed in the hostile home atmosphere. Therefore, the Pentagon replied with advice to tone down the message.

Whereupon, as Ellsberg told the story, cables flew back and forth between Saigon and Washington until an agreed-upon scenario had been reached. This scenario was the contrived propaganda that Westmoreland and Bunker, through a gullible American press, had fed the public in 1967. Ellsberg apparently thought his "leak" would be enough to produce headlines in the *Times*. When I told him we'd need copies of the telltale cables to support his story, he protested that the cables were top secret; he believed (probably erroneously) that he could go to jail if he were caught disclosing them.

The upshot of the incident was that Ellsberg couldn't, at least didn't, produce the cables, and we never published his story — though I believed then and still do that it was true. It had been drummed into me, for all of what was then a 20-year newspaper career, and I still believe, that honest journalism requires confirmation — documentary backup if possible — before a story can be published.

At the time, Ellsberg didn't seem to realize the importance of confirming documents, but he may have taken the lesson to heart. At any rate, I believe he had taken the first step toward release of the Pentagon Papers.

Some years later, when I was no longer bureau chief but still a Washington columnist, I was working late in the *Times* bureau when Neil Sheehan walked into my office. I knew and admired him for his brilliant work on the ground in Vietnam, both before and after active U.S. participation in the war. Sheehan was a bulldog reporter who had to be cajoled and sometimes browbeaten into writing a story rather than endlessly seeking one more source, one more fact, one more quotation.

That night, Sheehan apparently feared — with some reason — that my office was bugged because he insisted that we walk around the bureau while talking. (In those days there was considerable paranoia about the FBI, the war and dissent.) So we did walk, traversing many times a corridor that surrounded the newsroom and offices. In little more than a whisper, Sheehan asked me if the *Times* would publish, if he could get hold of it, a top-secret history of U.S. involvement in Vietnam, compiled by Pentagon officials during the Johnson administration. The duplicity, official lies and mistakes it would disclose, he said, were so explosive that publication might actually make it impossible for the Nixon administration to continue the war.

I thought immediately of Dan Ellsberg and of our aborted effort to obtain and publish those Pentagon-Westmoreland cables. But Sheehan, conscientiously protecting his source or sources, refused to admit or even hint that Ellsberg was in any way involved. He also didn't tell me, though I know now, that he either already had the history in his possession or was sure he soon would have it. Thus, I knew neither that the story was available nor the source; so I could not let the cat out of the bag, which may well have been Sheehan's intent.

I was excited at the prospect Sheehan raised, but I knew I had no authority on such a matter and thus had no way to answer his question. I advised him to talk to James Reston, who was still the ranking Washington columnist, the patriarch of the bureau and a man who wielded vast influence in the New York office.

"If Reston says publish," I told Sheehan, "they may or may not do it. But if he says 'don't publish,' I guarantee you they won't."

That was the end of the matter, for me.[5] But Sheehan took my advice and went next to Reston. Scotty favored publication, as I had been confident he would. The whole matter then moved out of the Washington bureau into the publisher's office.

There is no need here for a detailed reconstruction of the story of the Pentagon Papers,[6] so I will just summarize some major events. Sulzberger, the publisher, decided to *prepare* the documents — all 7,000 pages of them — but to reserve judgment on whether to *publish* them. A hush-hush operation went on at the New York Hilton, where Sheehan, E. W. Kenworthy and other *Times* reporters whipped the papers into publishable shape. The venerable law firm of Lord, Day and Lord warned against publication of top-secret material and ultimately refused to defend the *Times* in court; the *Times* subsequently engaged different legal counsel. Tense arguments occurred within the staff and with the publisher about whether to publish the papers and, if so, whether to reproduce classified documents verbatim. Finally, Sulzberger made the bold decision to do both.

After three days of publication, the Nixon administration obtained a court order enjoining the publication of further articles, even though it was the Johnson administration's deceptions and missteps that were

---

[5] I later learned that Sheehan took the trunkful of documents to Bill Kovach, then the *Times* bureau chief in Boston and later the curator of the Nieman Foundation at Harvard. Kovach managed to have the documents secretly Xeroxed and later told *Editor & Publisher* (Feb. 20, 2000, pp. 22-3) that his clandestine association with this "great story" was one of his proudest moments.

[6] Those who want a fuller account will find it in *The Trust: The Private and Powerful Family behind The New York Times,* by Susan E. Tifft and Alex S. Jones (New York: Little Brown & Co., 1999). Jones has been appointed to succeed Bill Kovach as the curator of the Nieman Foundation.

being exposed. The *Times* obeyed the order but appealed the decision, and the matter rose on a fast legal track to the Supreme Court. The Supreme Court decided unanimously that the administration's attempted "prior restraint" was unconstitutional; publication could proceed. One of the pillars of American liberty — freedom of the press — had been resoundingly upheld, and so had the *Times'* courageous though reluctant decision to rely on it.

Such an outcome was by no means certain when the question of the Pentagon Papers was first put to Arthur Sulzberger; he thought that it "smelled of twenty years to life."[7] Louis Loeb, of Lord, Day and Lord, counseled that publishing top-secret material would be a crime. One of his partners was none other than Herbert Brownell, who as attorney general in the Eisenhower administration had helped devise the classification system the *Times* proposed to violate. No one at the *Times* could be sure of what would happen, but many believed that Loeb was wrong. Nor could anyone be sure how the courts would rule, even though the classification of the documents had not been established by law but by executive order. Furthermore, no one could say for certain how the public would react. Would the public support such defiance of government classification, or would publishing government secrets ruin the *Times'* reputation for probity?

Strong voices within the paper's own bureaucracy, notably including that of Harding Bancroft, an executive vice president and former State Department official, either opposed publication or warned of dire consequences. To this day, many Americans believe the *Times* was wrong to traffic in "stolen property" (although charges against Ellsberg ultimately were dismissed). Others think, so they tell me, that the *Times* only wanted to sell papers. In fact, there was no spectacular circulation gain during this period, and given the legal costs it incurred, the *Times* actually lost money by publishing the Pentagon Papers.

President Nixon, after initial hesitation, heeded the advice of his national security adviser, Henry Kissinger. They loudly proclaimed (as did their representatives in federal court) that the government's necessary ability to keep secrets had been destroyed, that no other government ever again could trust Washington, and hence that important foreign policy operations could not be conducted. Nearly 30 years later, no evidence exists to support these charges, and the Nixon administration's solicitor general has admitted that there was no hard evidence in 1971 either — only Kissinger's fears.

---

[7] *The Trust,* p. 483.

Arthur Sulzberger, who properly assumed the burden of making the final decision about publishing the Pentagon Papers, had no rule book or code of ethics to guide him. Nor were there any clear precedents. He heard conflicting advice from persons he trusted — from Bancroft and Reston, for instance, and from Louis Loeb and James Goodale, the *Times'* in-house counsel. Conventional wisdom outside journalism, and to a surprising extent within, argued against publishing "stolen" secrets. No one, of course, advised Sulzberger to be irresponsible; the question was, what *was* responsible?

It's easy, when dire predictions have failed to be borne out, to see in retrospect that Sulzberger did do the responsible thing in 1971. It wasn't easy at the time, though, for him, his advisers or for outside observers. He did have one semi-imperative: He knew that if he refused to publish, after the *Times'* partial submission to the government in the Bay of Pigs case, journalists in general would be disgusted and quite a few *Times* editors and reporters might well resign in protest. Some would have.

He also knew, however, that if he did publish and the courts then ruled against the *Times,* a heavy fine could follow, a large part of the general public might regard the paper's action as near treason, and the principle of a free press might be irreparably damaged.

Few other publishers or editors have faced a single choice of such magnitude. Nevertheless, all journalists have to cope with lesser but still crucial decisions day after day, year after year. In most cases, they have no clearer guide to follow than the *Times* had in 1971.

Many nonjournalists who recognize the influence of the press, both broadcast and print, on all kinds of events urge the adoption of a code of ethics for journalists. Quite a few practicing reporters and editors take that position, too. Lawyers have such a code, it's often pointed out, and public confidence in journalism would be enhanced if there were a known set of do's and don'ts against which actual press performance could be measured.

These arguments *seem* plausible, even compelling, and of course it's hard to argue the other side: to appear to be against ethics, responsibility, and good citizenship. Nevertheless, since I entered journalism in 1949 as editor, reporter, ad salesman and Omaha folder[8] operator of

---

[8] A device for folding and cutting a large square of newsprint into an eight-page newspaper.

the *Sandhill Citizen* (circulation about 1,800 a week) of Aberdeen, N.C., I have opposed a code of ethics for journalists, and I still do.

This may seem strange, considering the argument already put forward that journalism has no comprehensive rules and that journalists often face hard choices with no real guidelines. In fact, however, that argument is the primary reason for my opposition to a code, a position that has earned me the disapproval of several respected journalists. I had many arguments on the subject with Lester Markel, who for many years was the so-called Sunday editor of the *Times* and the originator of the book review, the "news of the week in review" and the Sunday magazine. I never convinced him, nor he me.

In the first place, I contend, journalism is not a profession like medicine or the law. One need not have a journalism degree or pass a professional examination or have a license to practice journalism. Such requirements would be incompatible with the freedom of the press enshrined in the First Amendment. That freedom means that anyone of any political persuasion, education, race, religion, sex or nationality can be an American journalist. If journalistic standards such as licensing or qualifying exams did exist, it would be too easy to find reasons true or false to bar persons in some or all of those categories.

A code of ethics, moreover, presupposes professional status. The only way such a code can be enforced is with the threat of suspending a license or expelling an offender from the stated profession. In professions like medicine or law, such threats, or actual suspension and expulsion, do not always work to enforce legal or other professional ethics codes. So how could a code for nonprofessional journalists require them to follow its dictates? Who should have the power to throw a reporter or an editor out of journalism? And if anybody did have that power, what would remain of freedom of the press?

Basically, then, I have two objections to a code of ethics for journalists. First, such a code would be a step toward converting the free craft of journalism into a licensed profession, which is incompatible with freedom of the press. Second, such a code could not be enforced because no one has, or should have, the power to remove, or even threaten to remove, a journalist from journalism (except perhaps in the case of actual crimes like theft or embezzlement).

The Ten Commandments are essentially a code of ethics for a nonprofessional group — for all of us. But does anyone contend that therefore we do not have among us murderers, thieves, adulterers and unbelievers? The Commandments, in fact, are also unenforceable except in the case of proven crimes. Even then, one goes to prison for violating the law, not one of the Commandments.

Furthermore, since journalism is not a profession, there is no authoritative body to set out a code of ethics for all — for print journalists, broadcasters, freelancers with their desktop publications, academics writing for the popular press, photographers, cartoonists, citizens contributing to the local weekly and so on. Numerous groups have tried to devise a code, but none has been able to speak for, much less regulate, all who call themselves journalists. Nor has any group had the power to enforce the code it has recommended.

An even more fundamental difficulty involves writing an actual code. Because journalists make such far-ranging and diverse choices, no code would likely encompass them all. An inadequate code would not only be of little help in most cases but could actually have a negative effect. If it did not cover a particular situation facing some journalist, he or she might reasonably conclude that the situation did not involve ethics at all. If journalists decide "it's not in the code," they might feel free to do what's most profitable or most popular. If, on the other hand, they have to ponder a choice in the abstract, without some inadequate code to check, they will be more likely to consider and observe the ethical dimension.

The impact of a journalistic code of ethics on public confidence in the press would, at best, be problematical. Suppose there were a code (despite the problems I've raised) and some journalists, for good reason, felt it necessary in particular instances not to follow it. Their violations, not their good reasons, probably would be publicized, even by journalistic colleagues. If, however, journalists' interpretations of the code led them to follow it into unpopular or disastrous actions, the code would provide scant protection.

Suppose, too, that in 1971 some code of ethics, official or otherwise, had persuaded Arthur Sulzberger not to publish the top-secret Pentagon Papers? It is doubtful that any code would have urged him to publish the government's supposed secrets.

In short, I believe there is no substitute for a journalist's integrity, sense of honor and desire to be responsible. A specific code of ethics is a poor replacement for any of those attributes. Codes enjoin caution, limit choices and invoke the conventional wisdom. They do not usually encourage bravery, risk-taking and challenging the status quo.

CHAPTER 2

Man Bites Dog?

What is "news," anyway?

The classic response — "man bites dog" — is sadly inadequate. It suggests that news is unusual, that it rarely happens. It further suggests that when news does happen, it belongs in a sensational tabloid, next to the Elvis sightings and UFO landings.

If, in fact, news is only "man bites dog," then news is not merely unusual; it's outside the normal course of human events. In other words, men don't bite dogs in any sane modern setting, like a neighborhood. The main thing that does happen in such surroundings is that people go about their daily work.

But everyday events aren't necessarily news either. If it's too narrow to define news as an extraordinary happening, it's too broad to say that news is *anything* that happens. In fact, news may be either or neither or both.

News doesn't even have to *happen,* as a murder or an election or a politician's speech happens. News can be something that *is happening,* but not just at a particular time or place, such as women having more children out of wedlock. News can be something *not happening,* too: no reported thefts last night, neither Barry Bonds nor Sammy Sosa hitting a home run yesterday.

Your local newspaper or nightly news broadcast certainly would include an item about a man biting a dog if your local journalists knew about that event, which they well might not. An imaginative reporter, on the other hand, might make an interesting story out of obscure people doing their often boring duty every day. That relative miracle is what life is mostly about.

If a man bit a dog on his way to work, that story would include both the unusual and the routine. Most of us, after all, only have to cope with the routines of traffic on the freeway or looking after the kids, not with chewing on canines.

News may also be, as some critics insist, whatever the person who owns a press *says* news is. Nowadays, though, those who own presses usually have little influence on what is going to be printed on them, and sometimes they don't even know. History tells us that William Randolph Hearst, who owned a lot of presses, dictated the "news" that led the United States into the Spanish-American War a century ago. And the courageous publisher of *The Washington Post*, Katharine Graham, certainly was saying what she thought was news when she authorized publication of the Pentagon Papers in the *Post* even after *The New York Times* had been enjoined from publishing by the Nixon administration and the courts.

> She was mid-toast at a dinner at her home when [Ben] Bradlee and other executives called. It was decision time. Graham hedged: Couldn't it wait? No, they said. She asked her lawyer and board chairman whether he'd publish if he was in her position. "I guess I wouldn't," he said. But her editors were pressing her: "You've got to do it."
> And so she did. "Go ahead," said Graham. "Let's go. Let's publish."
> . . . [T]hat moment made a serious national paper out of the *Post*.[1]

Publishers and broadcast executives differ, of course, as widely as Katharine Graham and Rupert Murdock, Richard Salant and Ted Turner. When I wrote a political column for *The New York Times*, the only instruction I had from the publisher, Arthur Sulzberger, was that I should not endorse a presidential candidate. Such an endorsement, Sulzberger decreed, was his prerogative, to be expressed in an editorial at his direction. Every other question or issue was open to me to write about.

To a considerable extent, news is what *editors* say it is. Editors become editors, in fact, because of their supposed "news sense." They like to say, and some even believe, that they can "smell a story." As a result, reporters often find themselves racing after obscure facts, false leads, uncooperative people, unwarranted assumptions.

Lester Markel once assigned me to do an article for the *Times* magazine on what he said was President Kennedy's method of collecting votes in Congress the way he had collected delegates to the Democratic National Convention in 1960. I went to see Kennedy and dutifully put this notion before him.

---

[1] Geneva Overholser, "Most Influential Newspaper People of the 20th Century," in *Editor & Publisher*, Centennial Edition, Oct. 30, 1999.

Puffing a cigar and shaking his head, the president told me he was "afraid your story's not there." He then delivered a cogent lecture on his actual methods of collecting votes in Congress. They had been none too successful, he conceded, in the heyday of the old Republican–Southern Democratic coalition.

Pleased with these words from the horse's mouth, I wrote what I thought was an erudite article based on them. Back came word from Markel: "No! I want a story about how Kennedy goes after votes the way he went after delegates to the convention."

I rewrote my piece but got the same rejection for the same reason. So I finally got the idea. In the third version, I was careful to include, near the beginning, something like this:

> Kennedy's approach to congressional votes is sometimes compared to his pursuit of delegates to the Democratic convention in 1960. The president does not concede this, only that he works hard to bring Congress to his point of view.

Then I detailed Kennedy's lecture to me.

Markel's response was succinct: "Great piece!"

Nevertheless, journalists and editors sometimes do smell news. James Reston relied heavily on his news sense. He'd pore over the morning paper and note (a) that something had been announced by the government. Then he'd read in an apparently unrelated story that (b) something else was going on. So if (a) and (b) were true, Reston reasoned (or sensed), then together they might mean that some unmentioned and unannounced (c) was true, too.

He'd then get on the phone to perhaps the secretary of state — high officials always took Scotty Reston's calls — and inquire in a deceptively casual manner about the probable (c) he had inferred from the morning paper: "I was just wondering, Mister Secretary . . . when did you decide to recognize Lower Slobbovia?"

In astounded tones, the secretary often would reply: "How did you know about *that*?"

Thus was news sometimes born in the intuition of a great journalist, to whom the astonished response was confirmation enough. Reston would then need only corroborating details to report the story.

If news is sometimes what publishers and journalists say it is, sometimes it is also what they don't even notice. For example, after World War II and the development of the mechanical cotton-picker, one of the great migrations of history occurred. Multitudes of black Americans — who had been ill-fed, ill-housed, ill-clad and ill-treated in the sharecrop South — departed for the industrial cities of the North and West. This immense population movement changed the nation forever, leaving many cities — Detroit is only one example — profoundly different.

Yet while this migration was going on, the newspapers and broadcasters of the time rarely reported it in any detail or with any understanding. Men were not biting dogs, it seems, on the Illinois Central from Mississippi to Chicago. More to the point, the nation's journalists didn't "smell" one of the great trends of the century. Instead, they were preoccupied with something those black people voting with their feet on the road to the promised land did not have: official spokesmen.

Spokesmen, that is, like Martin Luther King Jr., Thurgood Marshall, Roy Wilkins, Andrew Young, John Lewis and other luminaries of the concurrent civil rights movement. They also reported on civil rights supporters in Washington: people like Jacob Javits and Hubert Humphrey in the Senate, and ultimately John Kennedy and Lyndon Johnson in the White House. These men, and women like Rosa Parks, were the activists and leaders in the civil rights movement. As such, they were figures recognizable to the press. Their actions and followings, speeches and votes, could be covered and regularly reported to the nation.

Coverage of the civil rights movement, therefore, was important and effective, particularly when television film showed the nation such horrors as police dogs and cattle prods being used against Americans seeking their constitutional rights in Birmingham and elsewhere. But in the long view of history, will the civil rights movement that was so well reported be accorded a national impact greater than the contemporary migration that was hardly reported at all?

The point here is not which of the two movements was most important. Instead, it is to suggest that official spokespersons or leaders can and often do make the difference between what is reported as news and what is disregarded. Press secretaries, public relations officials, famous leaders and spin doctors can sometimes "make the news."

Consumerism, for instance, was not much talked about until Ralph Nader became its hard-hitting spokesman and aroused the attention of the press. The publication and success of Rachel Carson's *The Sea Around Us* led to a widespread, continuing environmental movement. And would the so-called Reform Party even have gotten on the 1992 ballot had not the colorful billionaire H. Ross Perot funded, fronted and represented it?

In fact, the recognized leader of almost any important national entity or movement — Henry Ford Sr. and William S. Paley in their time, NFL Commissioner Paul Tagliabue, Betty Friedan, Jesse Jackson, Bill Gates, Trent Lott, Colin Powell, the presidents of major universities, not to mention the man in the White House — can "make the news" virtually anytime he or she chooses to speak. Because such leaders are highly recognizable, the press pays attention to them and to those they're speaking for.

Unfortunately, many lesser lights may be just as important or official but are not so easily recognized by the press. Suppose someone is the representative of a national group advocating higher salaries for teachers. If the representative is not well known, the press may pay little attention to him or her, to an organization the press considers relatively unimportant and to its cause. For this reason, many such groups often seek sports or entertainment stars, such as Michael Jordan or Madonna or professional football players, to be their spokespersons.

The timing of reporting is important as well — not necessarily when a possible news event does or doesn't happen, but when editors or broadcasters or both decide to notice it and call it to public attention. The text of an earth-shaking speech may be available well ahead of time, but the press almost always observes whatever release date the author prescribes for the speech.

Many press organs impose on themselves a rule *not* to publish certain information, such as the name of a rape victim or a juvenile offender. The ostensible motive, in such cases, is to avoid embarrassment to a supposedly blameless person or to someone perhaps too young to be responsible, who might yet become a good citizen.

Such rules are general, though disputed among journalists. Is it fair to print this embarrassing fact but not that one, to protect A but not B? Would the press submit to such rules (amounting to censorship) if they were imposed from outside? Should it? Despite pious press pretensions, rules like these are violated almost immediately if some other outlet discloses the information first.

For example, many publications and broadcasters refused to use the name, though it was known, of the woman alleged to have been raped by William Kennedy Smith in Palm Beach in 1991. Once her name was published by one newspaper, however, much of the rest of the press — including *The New York Times* — quickly advertised her identity, too. Thus, in originally withholding her name, the *Times* and the others were not adhering to a principle; they were waiting only for someone else to break the supposed rule so that they could follow with a certain bogus impunity. They were waiting, it's fair to say, only for an excuse, however shaky.

In the case of the *Times,* something like a staff revolt followed its disclosure of the woman's name. In an attempt to justify their action, Executive Editor Max Frankel and his staff were forced to call a news department meeting in a large auditorium in the *Times* building. By all accounts, they did not make many converts. Most *Times* journalists obviously did not approve of what the paper had done. Just as obviously, the editors did approve — or they wouldn't have done it.

In short, it's hard to say what *is* news and it's equally hard to say what's *not* news. It is perhaps best to accept the idea that in certain circumstances almost anything may or may not be news. Keep in mind that the more important journalistic questions don't really concern what's in the press or what's not. Instead, good journalists ask *why* some particular information was published or broadcast or why it wasn't, *who* made the decision and *on what grounds*.

It's actually easier to distinguish among the *types* of information that get into print or on the air than it is to come up with a general statement about what news is or is not.

Hard news, for example, is basically an account of something someone considers important that definitely has happened. For newspapers, hard news could have happened yesterday or before; for broadcasters, it could have happened anytime before they went on the air.

Hard news is not speculative; it is an actual event: A politician spoke or issued a statement, a head count was taken in the legislature, the president signed a bill. By its nature, hard news can't be secret, either. In most cases, in fact, hard news either has been planned or prepared in advance, like a politician's speech, or is merely expected action, as when the president or governor approves or vetoes legislation, or when an unsuccessful candidate withdraws. The actors in the drama usually want maximum publicity, or, if they don't, they know that this particular hard news is so important that some exposure can't be avoided. An example is the defeat of a treaty in the U.S. Senate. So they don't even try to keep it quiet even if it's personally damaging.

Sometimes, hard news can nevertheless be a surprise, as when a candidate suddenly withdraws or a chief executive vetoes rather than signs a bill (or the other way around). Generally speaking, however, hard news is the plain record of an open past. It's often generated, timed and sometimes exaggerated or minimized by spokespersons, as when a member of Congress announces a federal grant for a local sewage plant or that she's been invited to visit the pope. But more often than not, hard news reflects what actually took place in the recent past.

Particularly abhorrent to me but frequent nonetheless, and sometimes unavoidable, is *horse-race* news. The analogy is to, say, a Kentucky Derby when the horses are in the backstretch. The race announcer is hard put to keep up with who's ahead, who's challenging, who's moving on the outside, and so forth. He certainly has no time to go into any horse's breeding, its jockey's record, how it's fared on similar footing, on tracks of greater or lesser length. That's for earlier or later reporting. When the race is on, the race itself — the moment, the action — is all the announcer has time to describe and all that listeners want to hear.

Horse-race news obviously is fine when a horse race has to be covered. But all too often, political, election and even international coverage tends to be too much like a race: Who's ahead? Who's challenging? What do the polls tell us?

In today's horse-race coverage of elections, little space is devoted to what the candidates may stand for, to what one result or another may mean to the voters, to the historical factors involved, or to *why* someone is winning or losing. In 1999 and 2000, although Al Gore and Bill Bradley made an issue of their differing health-care plans, it's safe to say that few voters learned from the press what the real differences between the plans were. Most coverage, instead, focused on whether Bradley had adequately answered Gore's charges, or vice versa — who was ahead?

As with that track announcer peering through his binoculars, to the political press nothing mattered but the race itself. The reporting may have been accurate but the larger understanding of the reader or the viewer — whose health-care plan does what? — was the loser.

A sort of horse-race journalism in reverse featured the extensive coverage of the Florida election results in the 2000 presidential race. (I was out of the country that excruciating November and followed the controversy mostly via the Cable News Network.) Since it was not clear whether George Bush or Al Gore finally would be accorded Florida's electoral votes (and the one who got them would become president), there was no traditional horse race to report. Instead, coverage was dominated by spokespersons — notably former secretaries of state James Baker for the Republicans and Warren Christopher for the Democrats — and by lawyers and legal interpreters. Bush supporters claimed that their man had won Florida under the state's existing election rules, which should not, in fairness, be changed after the fact. Gore's backers insisted that their favorite would have won if, in fairness, all the state's popular votes had been counted properly in the first place. In fact, the contest was less a principled dispute on such lofty matters than a straight-out, partisan power struggle over who would win the presidency.

This raw, underlying fact was seldom made clear in the coverage I saw. The press, for once, and of necessity, focused less on who had won, or was winning, or finally would win — since the race was over and the horses were in the barn — than on the empty claims of both sides to be the possessors of virtue and legitimacy. Not only did the Republicans finally win Florida's electoral votes and thus the presidency for Bush; but, to my mind, their televised "spin" was more nearly accepted by the press — thus contributing substantially to the nation's quick acknowledgment of Bush as president.

Breaking news is hard news that is usually unexpected and often happening right now, such as a long-dormant volcano erupting, a dramatic military movement, surprising election returns, a coup d'etat in the Third World.

I was covering breaking news in Dallas on Nov. 22, 1963, because President Kennedy's murder was certainly unexpected, and in the hours following his death more and more details became available. I also was covering breaking news the night President Johnson told the nation via television about a supposed, but probably nonexistent, Tonkin Gulf incident that became a milestone in the Vietnam War. Again, his totally unexpected announcement of his retirement from the 1968 presidential election was truly breaking news, especially at nearly midnight on an otherwise uneventful Sunday evening!

Wire-service reporters have to be — and most are — particularly adept at covering breaking news. Their reputations often depend on getting their stories on the Associated Press wire before the United

Press International correspondent files his or her account (or vice versa).

Only a moment after he saw President Kennedy shot in Dallas, the UPI's veteran reporter Merriman Smith, who was (according to seniority) in the front seat of the press pool car, seized the car telephone, threw himself with it under the dashboard, curled around the phone protectively, and dictated the historic bulletin for which he was awarded a Pulitzer Prize. As he dictated, another veteran, Jack Bell of the AP, is said to have been leaning over from the back seat, trying vainly to grab the phone away from Smith so he could file his own story. Had Bell been senior and in the front seat that day, he'd almost certainly have acted as Smith did.

Even in less trying circumstances, wire-service reporters often have to dictate a breaking-news story directly, under the pressure of time, without first having written it on paper. This is a skill most contemporary newspaper reporters, with the day of the "Extra" long gone, rarely have to call upon. In Dallas, unlike Smith and Bell, whose services had to move the story on the wire immediately, I had several hours before my first-edition deadline. Radio and TV reporters, of course, often tell their stories directly to the microphone and camera without having written them first.

The only time I had to dictate a breaking story directly was in 1962 before President Kennedy's death and while the Cold War was still a headline matter. Along with other reporters, I was called by Pierre Salinger, the presidential press secretary, at about 2 a.m. and told to come to the White House as soon as possible. Shortly after I arrived, Salinger announced that the United States and the Soviet Union were at that moment making a prisoner exchange that would free Francis Gary Powers, the American U-2 pilot who had been shot down on what turned out to be a spy mission over Russia. As Salinger spoke, Powers was being released on a bridge between sectors in Berlin (which accounted for the early hour of the announcement in the United States).

This was breaking news indeed, and sensational news in the Cold War atmosphere of 1962. But the *Times* first edition was already off the press and the final edition was rolling; I had no time to do anything but grab a phone and dictate off the top of my head. The New York office cooperated splendidly, and the next day I was gratified to learn that we'd made thousands of final-edition papers with a reasonably coherent and grammatically correct story. (Rewrite editors no doubt had done yeoman work on my hastily dictated prose.)

Later in the morning, I learned to my dismay that Kennedy himself had leaked the story of Powers' release to Ben Bradlee of *Newsweek,* his personal friend. Bradlee phoned the news to *Newsweek*'s sister publication, *The Washington Post,* in ample time for the *Post* to get a complete story into most of its editions. *C'est la guerre* — and journalism.

An *exclusive* story is one that appears only in one newspaper or on one broadcast. It's sometimes of sufficient importance that other news organizations have to follow it with a catch-up story of their own.

Little can give a reporter more satisfaction than digging up an exclusive — not because it's necessarily such a great story or a great public service but because a reporter, like any competitor, wants to be first, in this case with the news. TV news departments sometimes boast in expensive ads or promos that *their* reporter was ahead of the network competition by as little as a few seconds.

Most exclusives are, in fact, mere early birds. That is to say, something that's going to become hard news on a Friday — a speech that will be made or a policy that will be announced — may become someone's exclusive on Wednesday or Thursday. An enterprising reporter may have dug up the facts before the speech or announcement has been made. Or a source, probably seeking the maximum effect for the hard news to come, has leaked the story in advance to a favored reporter, perhaps in return for a guarantee of page-one exposure in a newspaper or lead-story status on television.

Sometimes, however, the source may want to spoil and counter the surprise, thus changing the calculated effect of the story. Either way, such an early-bird exclusive appears before the planned hard news, and its author gains an advantage over competitors who have to wait for the official event to try to catch up.

I once wrote an early bird that stayed exclusive for less than a day. I had learned by subterfuge that President Kennedy was about to nominate John McCone to be the new director of the Central Intelligence Agency. As soon as the *Times* published my story, however, Salinger made the official announcement and the story then appeared everywhere. *Sic transit gloria.*

Some exclusives, however, are more than early birds and therefore give reporters even greater satisfaction than that of merely being first. In such cases, the exclusive will have been developed from sources private to the reporter involved and concerns information that probably never would have been made public had the reporter not unearthed it. Readers and viewers, for example, might never have known the story of President Clinton's sexual affair with a White House intern had it not been for an exclusive on the Internet.

I had little to do with the exclusive I remember with the most satisfaction. A team of reporters in the Washington bureau of the *Times,* when I was its chief, toiled for days doggedly and brilliantly to put together a dynamite story during the Vietnam War. In the wake of the North Vietnamese "Tet" offensive in 1968, U.S. headquarters in Saigon was requesting that President Johnson send 486,000 American troops as reinforcements for the roughly half-million soldiers already in Vietnam. The request was a tightly guarded government secret until our reporting team discovered it.

The subsequent disclosure on the front page of the *Times* was big news that horrified much of the nation and probably did as much as any single story to turn the American public against the war in Vietnam. The *Times* published the exclusive in a Sunday edition, so it appeared in New York just after 9 p.m. on the previous Saturday night, which, coincidentally, was the night of the annual Gridiron Club dinner in Washington.

Every major print reporter (no broadcasters then were allowed in the haughty Gridiron) and high official in the city, as well as many of the nation's leading publishers and political figures, were present at the dinner in the Capital Hilton Hotel. I watched in frank satisfaction as the news of the *Times'* sensational exclusive spread rapidly among the white-tied diners and as distinguished journalists rushed off on that late Saturday night to try — mostly without success — to match our story.

An exclusive, however, is not always such a triumph. Even C. P. "Peck" Trussell, who won a Pulitzer Prize while reporting for *The Baltimore Sun* and later worked with me in the Washington bureau of the *Times,* liked to tell, albeit ruefully, about a story he'd written for the *Sun.* It turned out to be so egregiously wrong, he said, that it "remained forever exclusive."

The risk of error is a prime hazard in working on a story with sources private to the reporter involved. Douglas Kiker, then of the *New York Herald-Tribune*'s Washington staff, once wrote an exclusive story that the FTC was about to be abolished. His source called him frantically the next morning.

"Doug," he shouted, "it's the F-Pee-C, not the F-Tee-C!"

Although the story turned out to be wrong either way, Kiker, a blithe soul, went on to do distinguished work for NBC-TV news.

Soft news is any of several varieties of stories, often on subjects of little intrinsic importance. Sometimes soft news involves an event or events that did not happen at a specific time or place but that journalists presume will be of value or of interest to readers. Some form of soft news frequently appears these days even on newspapers' front pages. It is also prominent in broadcasts, as editors seek to provide relief from the hard, often grim news surrounding it. The late, lamented Charles Kuralt specialized in soft news — sometimes, by conventional standards, not news at all — in his remarkable *On the Road* series for CBS-TV.

A *backgrounder* is a soft-news account gathered after a previously reported event. It purports to tell *how* and *why* the event happened and perhaps what the consequences of the event may be, if these have become clearer after the original happening. *The New York Times,* with its numerous correspondents and bureaus, makes a specialty of such backgrounders.

A few days after the U.S. Senate rejected the Comprehensive Test Ban Treaty in 1999, for example, the *Times* Washington bureau contributed a long, unsparing description of how and why and when Republican senators had targeted the treaty for defeat. The story made clear that an unsuspecting Clinton administration had believed, until too late, that Senate approval was routinely forthcoming. The piece had been put together by cooperating reporters covering both executive and legislative branches, and its lack of partisanship made it doubly devastating for a White House that appeared to have been asleep at the switch on a highly important issue.

A *feature,* on the other hand, is soft news that has no particular importance to the chronological record. It may be no more than a cute account of a dog returning home after two weeks' absence and the family's resulting joy. It may be as sober as a statistical report on the increasing incidence of teen-age suicide or an analysis of the fat component of the American diet.

A favorite feature is an emotional record of a onetime bad guy's conversion to the straight and narrow. For the purposes of such a feature, a story about a religious conversion often works best. Another popular feature is a story about someone in an unusual occupation.

Kuralt could have taken out a patent on this kind of feature. The survivor of a freak accident or the perpetrator of a bizarre deed often rates a feature. So does a raccoon in somebody's toilet — a feature I actually remember from my days on the *Winston-Salem Journal* in North Carolina.

Feature readers or viewers may enjoy or even need a personality profile of someone in the hard news, such as the man who pulled off a Third World coup or someone mentioned as a presidential possibility. They may want to know why the first lady (of the United States or, say, California) changed her hairstyle or why a particular senator spends his weekends as an officer in the Air Force Reserve. A feature can be almost any story calculated to interest a reader or a viewer, even if the subject would not ordinarily be judged newsworthy.

News-you-can-use is a category of soft news developed rather recently, as the emergence of television sharpened competition for readers and viewers. News-you-can-use is designed to be specifically and practically helpful. It may tell people about current movies, name the best olive oil among several tested or give instructions on how to keep household items in working condition. News-you-can-use may also tell readers or viewers how to get rid of cockroaches, cook exotic dishes, lay out a flower bed or eliminate crabgrass — virtually anything editors believe readers and viewers need or want to know.

Is news-you-can-use therefore really news? Maybe not. But it has become prominent in today's publications and broadcasts.

The preceding discussion of hard and soft news applies only to the so-called news hole, the larger part of a newspaper or a radio or TV report that is devoted to supposedly objective reporting. The stories that appear in the news hole, whether about yesterday's coup or about the White House cat, are supposed to be nonpartisan.

Tucked away in all newspapers, however, is a page or two devoted to editorial purposes. In broadcasts, editorials may be given a few minutes of air time. In newspapers' editorial and Op-Ed[2] sections, opinions and attitudes are not only permissible but are the stated purpose of the articles. Within these sections are the "Letters to the Editor" sent in by readers and at least two other kinds of pieces: editorials and columns.

---

[2] Op-Ed refers to a page opposite to, or across from and facing, the actual editorial page.

An *editorial* is the open and specifically stated opinion or advocacy of those who own or at least control the newspaper or broadcast agency, which might be a family, corporation, partnership or individual. When the *Los Angeles Times* or the *St. Louis Post-Dispatch* advocates passage or defeat of a piece of legislation, supports or opposes a candidate or a civic project, it does so in an editorial. Usually, two or three editorials appear in a typical newspaper edition, but only one appears in a typical broadcast.

Most news agencies have a specialized staff to write editorials, though these writers are seldom allowed to contradict the publisher or owners. Depending on the skill of that staff and the strength of the views expressed, editorials may be pungent or bland, influential or of little importance. At their best, editorials take a definite position, coming down squarely on one side of an issue or the other. Editorials, however, are seldom at their best. All too often, writers shy away from decisiveness and take a middle-of-the-road approach, using headlines like "The Road Ahead" or "Voters Must Choose."

While an editorial is supposed to express frank advocacy, a *column,* at least in my definition, is less advocacy than commentary. A column is more nearly a discussion of a proposition than an opinion about it, even though the author's point of view on the matter may be obvious.

Newspapers have long published editorial pages and columns. Now commentary and even advocacy are being heard more and more on television and radio. Eric Sevareid of CBS was one of the most graceful practitioners of commentary and advocacy, as was John Chancellor of NBC-TV. Bill Moyers of public television still is.

As some readers may recall, I was for 25 years a columnist appearing on the Op-Ed page of *The New York Times.* For most of that period, I wrote three columns a week (toward the end of it only two), usually about economic and political, sometimes international, questions. My point of view surely was apparent in most of those thousands of articles, and I never tried to conceal it. But I did not wish nor try to be only an advocate. In other words, if my column persuaded or alienated anyone, I wanted it to do so because of the persuasive power of the commentary, not just because someone agreed with or opposed my position on an issue. I thought it was my obligation to discuss an issue fairly, even if from a point of view, and to let the reader make a considered judgment, just as one opinionated person might after a give-and-take discussion with another.

As I mentioned earlier, in my quarter-century as a *Times* columnist I received only one specific instruction from the publisher, Arthur O. Sulzberger — not to endorse a presidential candidate. I saw no reason ever to question his decree. If it mattered, a reader easily could deduce my view as between, say, Jimmy Carter and Ronald Reagan in 1980. There was no need, save vanity, for me to state my preference baldly, and I never did.

No one would deny that a president's election or an earthquake in Turkey or a change of government in Britain is news — hard news, sometimes even breaking news. Such stories, in fact, are what most people think of as news. Yet soft news is becoming more and more important in the age of cyberspace and the Internet. In my judgment, soft news may well be the salvation — if there is one — of newspapers.

Because television news and to some extent radio have become the prime purveyors of hard, breaking news, the traditional newspaper is becoming obsolete. Newspapers are too slow, inflexible and limited in impact. The contrasts between newspapers and broadcast news have become particularly striking since the deployment of communications satellites. The speed, reach and immediacy of broadcast news and its ability to follow the chronology of events both near and far have rendered printed journals largely inadequate to the modern era of instant communications.

Consider the day after a presidential election. A typical newspaper subscriber might read the morning paper over breakfast at 8 a.m. But the headlines in the paper will be an accurate description of the situation seven hours earlier, at about 1 a.m., which is the last-edition deadline of many newspapers. What may have happened since then could have changed circumstances drastically; the candidate who was winning the election at 1 a.m. may have been hopelessly defeated by 8 a.m.

A person who had stayed awake into the early morning hours, however, would have been able, via broadcast news, to follow the curve of events as they unfolded. Such a watcher or listener would be more up-to-date at the breakfast table. If late election returns changed the result, TV or radio would have made that change apparent long after newspapers had sent out their final editions with outdated information.

The preceding scenario is typical — and not just on election night — of what is happening to newspapers as broadcast news reaches with immediacy and impact into infinitely more houses and families than even the highest-circulation newspaper can hope to touch. Broadcast news can reach even the most remote and isolated corner of the nation, and its reports are more up-to-date and often more dramatic because they are immediate. This is why broadcast journalism has, in effect, superseded the front pages of newspapers.

It is also why those newspapers that survive the broadcast challenge and the competition of the Internet will turn — already are turning — to soft news. They are writing not just cute features but the kind of backgrounders that tell readers why something happened, how it was managed, why decisions were made, and what the resulting new circumstances may mean to those affected.

Today, few newspaper readers need to know the outcome of last night's game or election or vote in the town council. They learned the result from late-night television or radio or the Internet. Similarly, fewer newspaper subscribers need to read at the breakfast table what happened yesterday because they've already been told by broadcast news in a more timely and dramatic fashion.

What they probably *don't* know from broadcast news is what newspapers most usefully can and should provide: insights and information about why events happen and what they mean.

CHAPTER 3

Bedrooms

On Sept. 4, 1997, a man named George Shinn visited his nephew at Absinthe, a drug rehabilitation center in Charlotte, N.C. George Shinn was a well-known figure who once had contemplated running for governor of North Carolina. Then 56, Shinn was the owner of the Charlotte Hornets of the National Basketball Association, Charlotte's first major-league sports team. His nephew introduced Shinn to another Absinthe client, a young woman involved in a divorce-child custody case.

Shinn and the woman seemed a mismatched pair; she was in rehab, and he was a leading Charlotte citizen. Shinn had made millions, first operating a chain of for-profit colleges and then expanding into real estate and an auto dealership. Married, with three children, he lived in the exclusive Seven Eagles subdivision and owned an expensive second house overlooking Lake Wylie, across the nearby state line in Tega Cay, S.C.

Though a millionaire, Shinn was not standoffish. After a friendly conversation with the young woman, he suggested that he might be able to get his own attorney, the well-known advocate Bill Diehl of Charlotte, to represent her in the divorce-custody case. She was delighted.

That night, Shinn — one of those persons who use the telephone like a third arm — called her to say that he had not been able to reach Diehl. However, the next morning, on Sept. 5, Shinn drove to Absinthe in a black BMW. According to the woman, he asked if she'd like to go with him to meet Diehl at Tega Cay. She agreed and they left together at about 8 a.m.

What happened from there on depends on which of the two you believe. It is what attorneys describe as a "he said/she said" case.

SHE: Shinn soon stopped at a gas station and called his housekeeper to tell her not to come to work that day. During the drive, he touched the woman's leg and breast; she told him to stop, and he did, saying that "he would be a good boy." Bill Diehl was not at the Tega Cay house.[1] After they arrived there, Shinn told her his wife was out of town, made several phone calls and then took her on a tour of the premises. In the master bedroom, Shinn pushed her down on the bed, grabbed her hair and forced her physically to fellate him. Afterward, she vomited. Shinn then drove her back to Absinthe and offered her $200, which she refused. Then, "he patted me on the knee and said we will do this again sometime."

HE (two years later, in court testimony): He never promised that Bill Diehl would be at Tega Cay, and it was the woman who made the sexual overtures, both in the BMW and at the Tega Cay house. In their first meeting on Sept. 4, she had sent signals that she was "available" and had agreed to meet him again. He conceded that at Tega Cay she had fellated him but said she had done so consensually and aggressively. Because her attorney had later offered to settle any controversy for $5 million, Shinn believed that the woman had set him up for extortion.

He told the South Carolina jury that he was "ashamed" and "embarrassed" by his "stupid mistake" but insisted, "I did not rape anybody."

Whatever happened at Tega Cay on the morning of Sept. 5, the people of Charlotte and the two-state area near the city, from which the Hornets draw their fans, did not immediately learn that *anything* had.

Not that the woman kept quiet. After Shinn took her back to the rehab center, she told counselors and others what she said had happened. That night, she told her estranged husband, who urged her to go to the police. Later that same night, she also told another man with whom — as it later developed — she may or may not have had sex. But she did not make a formal complaint to the police until Wednesday, Sept. 10, five days after the alleged attack at Tega Cay.

On Friday morning, Sept. 12, *The Charlotte Observer* (a morning daily in the Knight-Ridder newspaper chain), knowing nothing of the woman's allegations to the Charlotte police, reported on the front page of a local-news section that South Carolina officers and the FBI were

---

[1] Because Shinn admitted driving her across a state line and she originally claimed that she had been under duress, the FBI briefly played a part in the investigation of the incident but not in the litigation that followed.

investigating "an allegation of sexual misconduct" at George Shinn's lake house. That house had been searched, the *Observer* said, on Wednesday night and on Thursday, Sept. 11, in the presence of Shinn's attorney, Bill Diehl.

No one would say exactly who was being investigated. A spokesman for the South Carolina State Law Enforcement Division (SLED) did say that "we have an allegation of sexual misconduct at [Shinn's] residence." But when asked specifically if the allegation was against the Hornets' owner, the spokesman replied, "I can't say if it's him or . . . anybody else." Shinn himself told the *Observer* that on the advice of Bill Diehl, he would say nothing.

Charlotte police said the allegation had been made by a woman on Wednesday, Sept. 10. They would not give details or identify the woman who had made it, and they said their report of her charges would not be released until those charges had been investigated.

Bill Diehl was quoted by the *Observer* in the Sept. 12 article as saying: "There may be a time to make a comment. It isn't today."

The "time to make a comment" was not to come for more than two years. But the fact that George Shinn was at least the focus and perhaps the target of the investigation quickly became reasonably clear. The *Observer* reported on its front page the next morning, Sept. 13, that on Sept. 12, the day the search at his lake house became public knowledge, Shinn's attorneys "persuaded a South Carolina judge to seal the search warrant and all other information regarding the incident."

Leland Greeley, the South Carolina lawyer who filed the motion for this gag order,[2] had informed the court that he was representing George Shinn. In his motion, however, he said only that it was filed on behalf of "John Doe" in connection with the claims of "Jane Doe." Release of the documents would "cause irreparable harm to John Doe," the motion said. But Judge John Hayes granted the motion only as a temporary restraining order and scheduled a hearing for Monday, Sept. 15, to determine whether to make it permanent.

Before Greeley sought and obtained the order in South Carolina, moreover, Charlotte police had released their incident report on the

---

[2] "This is another example of somebody attempting to keep the public out of the process to try to gain an advantage," said Jay Bender, a lawyer for the South Carolina Press Association. "When you close the door to court records, there is no guarantee the public interest is being served."

still-unnamed woman's charges. They said the report was related to "the Shinn investigation." The report gave a brief version of her story (as outlined previously) but neither corroborated nor refuted it.

Shinn's principal attorney, Bill Diehl, tacitly confirmed the shocking news that the Hornets' owner was being investigated for sexual misconduct. As Diehl told the *Observer:*

> This may all sort itself out and nothing happens. . . . If nothing happens, to spend a lot of energy discussing this in the press hurts people. . . . It's not a public event. It's unfair to have this investigation suddenly a public event.

At the Sept. 15 hearing on his gag order, Judge Hayes ruled against Shinn's attorneys. He accepted the arguments of the press that the temporarily sealed documents were public records and that "somebody who may be rich and famous" should get "the same treatment as someone who is not."

Judge Hayes' cancellation of the gag order and the release of the previously sealed documents on Tuesday, Sept. 16, made it seem as if a window had been opened or a faucet turned on. In the *Observer* for Sept. 17, a glaring page-one headline read:

SHINN FORCED SEX ACT AT HOME IN S.C.,
WOMAN TOLD POLICE

Under the headline, reporters Liz Chandler and Gary Wright (assisted by four other staff writers) laid out Jane Doe's allegations to the police but still did not name her. The reason was given in the seventh paragraph of the story: "The *Observer* does not identify victims of alleged sexual assaults."

Presumably startled readers thus definitely learned for the first time that a family man regarded as a model citizen, a man who had put Charlotte into big-time sports, a man who had spoken and written about civic responsibility and religious values, was being accused of generally condemned behavior — if not yet of a crime. They did *not* learn the identity of the accuser, and they heard nothing from Shinn himself. The reporters did, however, quote an unhappy Bill Diehl "up high" (toward the beginning) of their story:

> It's entirely possible that when the investigation is complete, there won't be a prosecution . . . there are two sides to every story. There is

a side of this story that Mr. Shinn will tell at the proper time. . . . We'll simply take our lumps today. It's painful.

The unidentified woman declined to comment further but had an attorney tell the press that she "stands by her story." The *Observer* was able to disclose two new details: that the woman had been a client at the drug treatment center because of an addiction to a prescription drug, and that her husband of seven years was suing her for divorce and seeking custody of their year-old daughter. (Her husband had signed the necessary papers on the day of the alleged Tega Cay assault, but before he learned of it.)

If the alleged incident actually had occurred, and if it had involved criminal behavior, it had taken place in South Carolina. (The alleged improper touching of the woman in the car, which would have taken place in North Carolina, was not likely to be construed as criminal.) Therefore, it became the province of Tommy Pope, the 35-year-old prosecutor in York County, S.C., to determine whether a crime had been committed and whether to charge George Shinn with that crime.

Despite his relative youth, Pope already had handled a nationally headlined case. He had prosecuted Susan Smith, the South Carolina mother who had confessed to drowning her two children in 1995. Pope quickly denied the speculation that had been aroused by the temporary gag order — that George Shinn would get special treatment.

"The police are certainly going to take measured steps but I hope that's what they do in every case," he said. "We don't want to treat [Shinn] better than anybody else, and we don't want to treat him worse."

Pope also said he'd "probably decide something in October."

As the first stages of this story unfolded in the *Observer* on Sept. 12–18 (the alleged incident had happened on Sept. 5), I was a visiting teacher at Davidson College, a small liberal-arts school just outside Charlotte within the *Observer*'s circulation area. One class I taught was composed of juniors and seniors interested in journalism, only a few of whom had any intention of pursuing it as a career. This class quickly made me aware that many students — of course, not all — disagreed with the *Observer*'s handling of the story.

These students thought the Sept. 17 headline ("Shinn Forced Sex Act at Home in S.C., Woman Told Police") was unfair, suggesting too strongly that Shinn actually had done what the woman alleged. Men and women students both disputed the *Observer* policy of not naming the victim of an alleged sex assault. Why, they asked, should George Shinn's name be in headlines while hers was kept secret, not for a legal reason but because of the newspaper's own decision?

In a broader sense, such students asked, why should the press make so much of a case in which there was as yet no official criminal charge and in which, as Bill Diehl had observed, there might never be a prosecution? They felt that the story was bound to damage George Shinn's reputation and future, even if ultimately he were proved innocent. Moreover, some students — particularly women — were already anticipating the wealthy Shinn's later contention that he had been set up for extortion. Many cited a then recent case in Dallas in which a woman had charged two Cowboys football players with sexual assault and then recanted and pleaded guilty to perjury.

All this, as the dates indicate, followed quickly on the death of Britain's Princess Diana in France and the allegation then current that the photographers chasing her car were partly responsible. Consequently, my class, like the general public, was in something of an antipress mood.

The *Observer,* meanwhile, was hearing some of the same complaints from its readers. On Sept. 19, Susan Stabley, referring to that headline, wrote in a Letter to the Editor that she supposed " 'woman told police' isn't nearly as exciting as . . . 'Shinn forced sex act.' " In another letter, Renee Moses claimed that George Shinn would be "irreparably harmed by the publishing of these allegations" and cited a need for "the media to learn to police themselves in determining what is newsworthy and what is just a coldhearted, calculated move to boost ratings or sell newspapers."

Other letters offered similar complaints. Don Winslow charged that "the mere fact that the *Observer* is printing this story with so little information is criminal." And Graham Gardner asked, "If you are so concerned [about fair treatment to everyone], then why don't you wait until all the facts are present before you report a story?"

In an editorial on Sept. 18, the *Observer* attempted to address these various issues:

> If the complaint may not lead to prosecution, why should the public know about it? Why not report the story only if the evidence leads to indictment and prosecution?
>
> The reason arises from a basic concept. . . . Government must be accountable to the people. Once the criminal justice system receives a

report of a crime, the matter ceases to be private. The public has an interest in watching the criminal justice system to ensure that it is working properly — that, in this case, it does not back off when a powerless woman makes a serious charge against a powerful man.

Already, the editorial suggested, the temporary gag order had "raised suspicions that a rich man was receiving special treatment."

As for withholding the woman's name, "in this case the court is not concealing it" but there was, the editorial contended, "a simple reason" why the *Observer* had chosen to do so: "Experience has shown that fear of publicity has deterred women from reporting sex crimes."

Moreover, the editorial continued, "the woman's name is included in the legal documents" and therefore was part of "the public record." Anyone interested could learn her identity by inquiring. "Laws requiring official documents and procedures to be open for public scrutiny," the editorial concluded, "are the best way to maintain confidence in government and to deter official misconduct."

This conclusion comes close, however, to forcing other questions: Didn't withholding the woman's name in itself violate the editorial's dictum that "official" matters should be "open for public scrutiny"? Doesn't every American have the right to face his or her accuser? When the facts were in dispute and it was possible no criminal case would result, wasn't the *Observer* allowing Jane Doe to hide from the supposedly required confrontation?

As for the newspaper's plausible assertion that fear of publicity often deterred sexual-assault victims from reporting the crime, Jane Doe already had gone to the police. Perhaps she might not have, of course, had she feared public identification. But some readers probably felt that, in fairness to George Shinn, the rule that guarded Jane Doe's identity should have been broken.

The *Observer* might well have replied that being "fair" to George Shinn in such a manner would have been, in fact, to grant him a privilege — the public identification of his accuser — denied to numerous others in the past. What made George Shinn deserving of "fairness" when other less wealthy, less influential persons had not deserved or received such a privilege?

The *Observer's* policy itself, rather than its specific application in the Shinn case, seems more questionable to me. Not identifying sexual-assault victims because such victims may not come forward if they fear publicity is a policy followed by many news organizations. It's extended by some organizations to juvenile offenders as well. In these cases, the policy is intended to prevent someone's juvenile offenses from prejudicing his or her later adult prospects.

In all too many instances, however, news organizations will breach the policy of nonidentification if some other newspaper or broadcaster does it first. The policy, then, is not so much a standard as it is a self-protective device to avoid criticism for doing a questionable thing before anyone else does it. But if it's questionable at all, isn't it questionable no matter why or when it's done? Why should *The New York Times* name a previously unidentified rape victim because some other paper in the Midwest or the South does so? The victim either deserves anonymity in the *Times* or does not; identification either is questionable or is not.

In the Shinn case, however, the *Observer* followed its policy consistently and did not name Jane Doe until she consented to an on-the-record interview. Therefore, the question seems to me not so much whether Doe's name was properly withheld by the *Observer* for more than a year but whether the newspaper's overall policy of not identifying sexual-assault victims is sound.

Although mine is the minority view, I believe that such a policy compromises the larger claim of journalism to print all the known facts without fear or favor, regardless of the consequences.

The most vexing and perplexing of privacy questions may be, who, if anyone, has a right to privacy?

Did George Shinn? Not after Jane Doe went to the police and after his Tega Cay house was officially searched. At that point, a public record existed and a criminal accusation had been made, sufficient to cast at least a shadow on the public face of civic and family virtue that Shinn had maintained. Had *The Charlotte Observer* ignored the public record (thereby concealing that shadow), it could have been accused of covering up for a rich and powerful civic leader. It also would have been accused, and rightly so, of abdicating its responsibility, betraying its claim to serve the public without fear or favor, and disregarding its obligation to truth (the truth that a charge had been filed).

It later turned out that Shinn was severely damaged by a charge from which no indictment arose. But that possibility was not properly a part of the *Observer*'s considerations. Neither were issues of competition and circulation, at least not in comparison to the larger questions of truth, obligation and responsibility.

In general, if news purveyors considered the consequences of what they publish or air as being equal to their obligations, they would more nearly be politicians than journalists. And quite a lot of vital information, in that case, never would reach the public.

Suppose, however, that the person in question is not George Shinn, or some even more "private" citizen, but the president of the United States? Suppose the president claims the right of privacy, as Bill Clinton did during his ordeal in 1998 and 1999?

Presidents and presidential candidates do not make a claim for privacy while they seek headlines, photographs, affection, admiration and votes by exposing every facet of their lives — religion, grief, pets, passions — even, for Clinton, underwear preference. If Al Gore had been elected president, after having exhibited to the public, on national television, the extent of his suffering over the death of his sister and over an accident involving his son, would he not have sacrificed what many would consider his personal privacy to his ambition?

Turn the question around. What right does a president or candidate have to personal privacy? Again I offer what is undoubtedly a minority view: very little.

He (someday she) wanted to lead, wanted the White House and voluntarily sought — in fact, fought hard, sometimes ruthlessly — for the privileges and responsibilities of the presidency, and wasn't forced to give up private life for public. Colin Powell, for one, and who knows how many other distinguished persons, refused to make the exchange.

The president accepts the pay, residence, expense accounts and emoluments of the office and will someday welcome an ex-president's handsome pension. He travels in luxury on *Air Force One,* asks for our trust in innumerable ways, and holds himself out as our national voice in international affairs. Frequently availing himself of what Theodore Roosevelt called the "bully pulpit," the president also plays the part of a national role model: scourge of the bad and exemplar of the good, a national cheerleader urging on the troops and the voters.

The so-called splendid misery of the presidency is, after all, splendid first. Why shouldn't the American people, who alone can confer that splendor on someone who has clawed his or her way toward it, demand to know all there is to know about that person? Why should they not know (even if it's too late to reject him) if the president is a liar, an abuser of women or of his position, cruel to subordinates and pets, in precarious health, careless about money or the Constitution, or concealing a sleazy past? All that and more could be covered up under expansive claims of privacy.

A few days after the *Observer*'s defensive editorial appeared on Sept. 18, columnist Jerry Shinn (presumably no relation to the Hornets' owner) spoke somewhat more pragmatically about the journalistic issues involving George Shinn:

> If we had ignored the story, which other local media would have aired, most readers surely would have thought either (a) we were trying to protect George Shinn, or (b) that we were so lazy and incompetent we didn't even know about it — in which case they might wonder why they should count on us for any news. . . . If we serve up our fair share of celebrity scandal, some readers will criticize us for sleaze-mongering even as they read every word and pant for more. If we stick piously to news you really need to know, but which even we must admit can sometimes be boring, a lot of you will turn to more entertaining sources of information. . . .

Then Jerry Shinn got to the heart of the matter:

> It's not so easy to be a responsible, respectable newspaper that reflects the world and the community all around it without publishing some things a lot of us would rather ignore.

Indeed it isn't easy. Newspapers and broadcast organizations urge and train reporters to seek the truth, or more to the point, to "find out what you can and tell what you know." Can they then qualify the truth by saying "except in certain cases," or "not if it's about sex," or "unless it isn't wholesome enough for the whole family"?

They can't if they expect to maintain credibility and their readers' trust. Newspapers and broadcast organizations usually insist they have a responsibility to "reflect the world and the community." They can't make this claim and then demonstrate in practice that some aspects of the world and the community are off-limits, privileged perhaps, too hot to handle, distasteful or impolitic.

As with any ideal, it is, of course, sometimes impossible to "tell what you know," no matter what it is, and let the consequences be what they may. But the ideal is better served by recognizing it than by discounting it in advance. If, in the grim exigencies of everyday practice, the ideal can't always be followed, I would still hold with the old

Southern saying: "Every tub sits on its own bottom." Every departure from the ideal, that is, should be judged on its own terms for what it is or isn't. Exceptions should not be judged by some pious abstraction like "good taste" or "decency," on the limits of which honest persons often differ.

Jerry Shinn was right that in the matter of George Shinn, the *Observer* "owed [its] readers . . . a responsible job of reporting as much of the truth about what had happened and was happening as we could find out." There was, after all, a public record, since Jane Doe finally reported her accusation to the police and George Shinn's lawyers ultimately failed to have it and other parts of the record concealed from the public by court order. Since that record did exist, the *Observer* would have been derelict in a newspaper's duty if it had not reported the story as soon and as fully as possible.

Whether the *Observer*'s actual reporting was responsible is another matter and one on which editors and readers can honestly disagree. Just as some of my students thought the coverage was unfair to George Shinn, other readers probably doubted that the newspaper was telling them "as much of the truth" about Shinn as it could find out. Still others probably sided with Jane Doe and considered the coverage of Shinn perfectly acceptable. Fairness, like beauty, always is in the eye of the beholder, who is seldom without a preconceived opinion.

In controversial press cases, however, it's not readers or viewers but editors and reporters — journalists — who have to make the decisions, provide headlines and stories, "play" them below or above "the fold," put them on page one or "back with the truss ads." In making such decisions, journalists can't refer to a comprehensive rule book compiled by infallible authorities; reporters and editors are not bankers checking interest rates in a printed guide. Nor can journalists take a poll of the public or, in many instances, even find guiding precedents to tell them what to do.

Like Turner Catledge watering down the Bay of Pigs story in the *Times,* editors have to act on whatever information they have and on their experience and background. They know that if they're wrong, they'll hear about it from readers — and sometimes from the law (or from the president of the United States, as Catledge did). Even when they're right, they'll hear from some readers who believe they were wrong.

Some of my objecting students at Davidson, for instance, considered themselves vindicated when the *Observer* disclosed on Oct. 3 that David Bland, a lawyer for the still unidentified (publicly) Jane

Doe, had suggested to Bill Diehl that George Shinn pay her $5 million. Bland said the money was to settle "civil issues" and that his proposal was a response to a suggestion from Diehl that there was "a small window of opportunity" for a settlement. Diehl vehemently denied making such a statement, leaving some with the impression, perhaps deliberately, that extortion had been attempted.

I tried to convince my class that there was no more reason to believe Diehl than Bland (he said/he said) and that, in any case, a settlement proposal from a supposed victim was not unusual. Nor was it implausible that George Shinn was willing to settle "civil issues," but not for $5 million. The lawyers' exchange, I insisted without much success, did not prove anyone's guilt or innocence of either an alleged crime or a supposed extortion.

Some "fairness" objections to the *Observer*'s procedures also seemed to have been validated the following month. On Nov. 22, more than two months after the alleged offense and well beyond Tommy Pope's self-set October target date, Pope announced that he would not bring criminal charges against George Shinn, or even refer Jane Doe's accusation to a grand jury, though he referred to her, perhaps inadvertently, as a "victim."

He believed, Pope said, "that something did, in fact, transpire between Mr. Shinn and this victim in Tega Cay. However . . . I do not feel that the state would be able to carry the burden of proving the case beyond a reasonable doubt."[3]

He stressed that George Shinn's influence in the community did not enter into his decision and insisted that 10 weeks did not represent a long delay in making it. But David Bland, describing himself and his client as "stunned," said he was already preparing a civil suit for damages against Shinn. Such a suit, the *Observer* properly noted, would require a lower standard of proof than a criminal charge.

The civil suit, alleging sexual assault, was filed on Feb. 6, 1998. On Feb. 12, George Shinn countersued Jane Doe for slander and extortion. And there, for another year, the matter mostly stood. Then, in an interview published in the *Observer* on Feb. 28, 1999, Jane Doe came forward to identify herself publicly as Leslie Price of Matthews, N.C., near Charlotte. At that point, she was 29 years old, reunited with her

---

[3] In April 1999, Tommy Pope reopened the case. On the basis of what he said was new evidence concerning Shinn and other women, Pope submitted the case to a South Carolina grand jury. That jury also refused to return an indictment against Shinn.

husband, and free of addiction to the prescription painkiller Darvon but a frequent victim of nightmares.

Every time she left her house, the *Observer* reported, she carried a 9 mm Glock handgun.

Here is a brief resume of the outcome of the Shinn-Price case:

Leslie Price's civil suit went to trial in Columbia, S.C., on Tuesday Dec. 7, 1999, more than two years after whatever happened at Tega Cay on Sept. 5, 1997. Shinn took the stand on the first day and finally told his side of the story. He denied all charges of criminal behavior, insisting that Price had been the sexual aggressor.

Early predictions that Shinn would be ruined by the disclosure in the *Observer* of Price's charges against him may have been, by then, at least partially borne out. In March 1999, he had moved from Charlotte, where he had once been a leading citizen, to Jupiter, Fla. That same month, his wife of 26 years filed for divorce, though her action reflected not only Price's charge but advance word of what had become official knowledge in a sworn deposition on June 18.

On that day, a former Hornet cheerleader — Jane Doe 2 — said in a deposition that she and Shinn had carried on a two-year sexual affair and that he had paid money to her.[4] In private life a Charlotte schoolteacher, as was later disclosed, Jane Doe 2 did not accuse Shinn of physical violence but said she had consented to the affair with him in fear that otherwise he would ruin her career. Telephone records showed Shinn had called Jane Doe 2 more than 20 times on Sept. 4, the day before he and Leslie Price went to Tega Cay.

Price's attorneys alleged that another Shinn sexual victim, Jane Doe 3, a former Hornets employee, existed. If so, she never testified, publicly or under oath.

Shinn sold 40 to 49 percent of the Hornets on July 28, 1999, for $80 million. Whether, therefore, he really was ruined, readers may judge.

Leslie Price also suffered at least mental distress in the years between Tega Cay and the trial. It was disclosed that she had used her podiatrist husband's medical credentials to obtain Darvon to feed her earlier addiction, sometimes taking as many as three dozen pills a day and more than 30,000 over seven years. She was accused of trying to

---

[4] It was this disclosure that caused Tommy Pope to refer the reopened case to a South Carolina grand jury, which refused to indict Shinn.

fake income-tax records and confessed to a brief affair, while separated from her husband, with another Absinthe client, ultimately identified as one Michael Angelette. He charged but she denied (he said/she said) that they had engaged in sex on the night of Sept. 5, only hours after the Tega Cay incident. Lawyers and experts for the two sides disputed whether, if Angelette's charge was correct, her alleged behavior that night would have been unlikely for a woman who claimed to have been a sexual-attack victim hours earlier.

Bill Diehl presented a loud and histrionic defense of George Shinn at the Columbia trial, which lasted 11 days. Price also told her story, denying Angelette's. Her case was presented by Vickie Eslinger, a South Carolina attorney who specialized in women's rights.

After closing arguments, the jury deliberated for an hour and 43 minutes. First they voted by 10 to 2 to reject Leslie Price's charge against George Shinn. Then, after further argument, they returned a unanimous verdict against her.

She "really didn't have much evidence," a male juror said later. Another suggested: "There were just too many questions about what happened in that bedroom." Still a third juror offered what might have been in the minds of many: "I think she probably did something she didn't want to — but I think she did it because she wanted something from it."

Leslie Price said she was glad, anyway, that she had "stood up" to a powerful rich man. Shortly after the trial, she announced that she would not appeal the verdict. Not surprisingly, George Shinn, the newly divorced resident of Florida, then dropped his slander and extortion suit. Cause and effect were denied all around.

Long before Leslie Price identified herself, the privacy issues raised by her charge were clear and being publicly debated in the *Observer's* two-state circulation area as well as in my classroom. The same issues long had been, and still are, debated elsewhere.

Many of the same questions, save that of the identity of those involved, became cocktail-party chitchat in 1998, when the affair between President Clinton and White House intern Monica Lewinsky became public. As a result of the affair, Clinton later was impeached (basically for lying about the matter), tried by the U.S. Senate, and then acquitted in 1999. The right to privacy of public persons, and the propriety of press invasions of that supposed right, also were widely debated after the auto accident in Paris in which Princess Diana was killed. As noted earlier, the photographers chasing her car were at first considered responsible for her death, though French investigators later discounted that charge.

Privacy issues, especially those related in any way to sex, are a constant problem for the press. Gary Hart's promising campaign for the Democratic presidential nomination in 1988 foundered on such matters. A potential speaker of the House, Robert Livingston of Louisiana, was forced to resign from Congress in 1998 because of disclosure of an earlier sexual affair. Resignations, on similar grounds, from public offices of all kinds are no longer surprising.

On the other hand, mere charges don't always result in resignations or election defeats, and certainly not in deaths. Persistent rumors during the 1992 presidential campaign that President George Bush had a mistress (in some rumors a woman's name was even mentioned) never surfaced in any plausible manner. Although these widely circulated rumors were never proven wrong, Bush did not appear to suffer politically from them. He even rebuked a reporter for bringing up what he suggested was neither true nor relevant to the election. Did investigative journalists do their job, which includes exploding untruths, or fall down on it? Or did they just shy away from an explosive story?

More significantly, President Clinton won acquittal in the Senate's impeachment trial of 1999 after he had admitted lying to the U.S. public and engaging in a sexual affair with Lewinsky. Largely owing to a booming economy, his standing in office did not suffer much, though his personal reputation did. He had been first elected in 1992, moreover, despite many rumors about his womanizing and a televised charge by Gennifer Flowers that he had carried on an affair with her while he was governor of Arkansas.

Clinton managed to survive that. But four years earlier, Senator Gary Hart of Colorado, at the time the front-runner for that year's Democratic presidential nomination, had had to drop out of the race after it was disclosed in the press that he was involved in a sexual affair outside his marriage.

What was the difference in the two cases? After Gennifer Flowers made her disclosure on television in 1992, I, for one, was convinced that Bill Clinton was finished politically. Nor was I alone in predicting a repeat of Gary Hart's 1988 fate. Many journalists agreed but, like generals, we were fighting the last war. Clinton not only survived in

1992 but was elected. The apparent differences in the Hart and Clinton verdicts caused much American soul-searching in public and private gatherings, and of course in the press.

Had the nation by 1992 become so callused about illicit sexual behavior, important voices asked, that it would no longer condemn even a presidential candidate's alleged relations with a woman not his wife? Was public decadence replacing public morality, as Jerry Falwell and others never tired of warning?[5]

Or had readers and viewers become so accustomed to press violations of individual privacy rights that they no longer were angered at the victims of such charges? Instead, did the public consider the violations so unfair and improper that they actually produced sympathy and support for those whose rights supposedly had been violated?

In fact, specific and significant differences between the Hart and Clinton cases helped Clinton to recover and contributed to Hart's political demise. For one thing, Clinton's dalliance with Flowers (partially admitted only many years later) had taken place well before the 1992 campaign. But Hart was caught red-handed, as it were, in his affair with a Miami model while he was waging a vigorous and apparently successful primary campaign.

In 1992, Clinton could and did deny, even if unconvincingly, Flowers' charge. In Hart's case, conclusive photographs existed, and were published, of the senator and the model cuddling on a boat appropriately, if coincidentally, called *Monkey Business*.

Perhaps of greatest importance is the fact that Clinton's wife Hillary supported his defense and even appeared with him on television to help refute Flowers' charge. Lee Hart, on the other hand, distanced herself from her husband. Ultimately, they divorced.

Probably unmeasurable, moreover, is the extent to which Democrats in 1992 were willing to overlook Clinton's transgressions (or believe his denials) for the sake of what looked as if it might become a strong Democratic candidacy. After all, the Democrats were fed up with 12 Republican years in the White House (and 20 out of what were then the last 24) and were facing an incumbent Republican, President Bush. By comparison, repudiating the enigmatic Hart in 1988, when no Republican incumbent would be on the November ballot (Ronald

---

[5] These questions predictably were revived in 1999, when Clinton was acquitted by the Senate of the impeachment charge based on his affair with Lewinsky.

Reagan after eight years as president was constitutionally ineligible), may have seemed to Democrats to be much less threatening to the party's prospects.

These differentiating factors, which may have determined the fortunes of two presidential candidates, had little to do with invasions of privacy. Nevertheless, the press still is often charged with crass violations of people's rights: *The Charlotte Observer* in the Shinn case, the paparazzi for Princess Diana's death, newspapers and broadcasters who seemed to be hounding President Clinton in 1998–99. In an earlier case of national notoriety, and of real journalistic culpability, the Supreme Court even found in the 1950s that press pressures had unfairly influenced the conviction of Dr. Sam Shepherd[6] in his first murder trial.

To some extent, of course, the response of readers and viewers in recent decades is part of a broader and more general animus against the media, which is not entirely irrational. In an era in which the news often was discouraging — about the Cold War with the Soviet Union, the threat of nuclear destruction, rising crime rates, race riots in the cities and racial discord everywhere — the messenger that brought these and other ill tidings had become more skeptical and challenging. Indeed, the media became more eager to expose official wrongdoing and more willing to report on matters such as sex (once considered taboo in a family newspaper) and national security (the sacred cow of patriotism). Added to this was the impact and reach of television news, which often magnified the impression of an irresponsible media. For all these reasons, the media were more disturbing and more controversial to readers and viewers, and therefore more suspect.

Supposed violations of privacy, however, may well have been and still may be the foremost cause of public criticism of the media. For every press exposure of such behavior as the alleged sexual harassment committed by Oregon's Republican Senator Robert Packwood, critics point to examples of press overkill. They argue against huge and invasive television stakeouts like the one in the front yard of Oliver North during the Irangate investigation of the Reagan administration. (In fact, the public seemed to resent this supposed invasion of North's privacy more than North himself did.)

* * *

---

[6] Shepherd, a Cleveland physician, denied, but was convicted of, murdering his wife. The later TV serial and movie *The Fugitive* were based on the Shepherd case.

I don't want to invade anyone's privacy — I value my own — and I particularly dislike stories about sexual misbehavior. I would not want to uncover and write such a story, and I deplore the tendency in today's press to emphasize — some would say exploit — sex.

Abe Rosenthal, once a brilliant reporter who later became the executive editor of *The New York Times,* has said that as an editor he would not have assigned a reporter to crouch outside Gary Hart's bedroom window and as a reporter he would not have accepted such an assignment. On other matters, I've often differed with Rosenthal; on this one, we agree. I once refused an assignment to cover an execution, and I would again.

These are personal preferences. I strenuously deny that anyone who seeks public office and public trust, particularly anyone who wins them — indeed, any person as public as George Shinn — has an automatic "right" to privacy. If it existed, this right, in my view, would be an immunity, like secrecy. It is neither to be found in the Constitution nor should it be granted by the press for anything less than a genuine showing that it's necessary and warranted.

This is yet another opinion not universally held among journalists, and it's certainly an assertion subject to question. But so are many of the decisions journalists may be and frequently are called upon to make. As with so many other such decisions, the best guide for practitioners is not likely to be found in a book or a code or an abstract principle but rather within themselves. The best guide for journalists is likely to come from a personal sense of what's right and what's responsible in that particular instance.

CHAPTER 4

Troopships

You're a reporter covering the White House or the State Department for a big-circulation newspaper or for one of the television network news departments. Following a tip from some trusted source, you manage to learn the following information. You have solid documentation, or confirmation from knowledgeable officials, but none of them, unfortunately, is willing to be identified as a source.

- An unfriendly nation is to be invaded by U.S. military forces at dawn on a certain date two weeks in the future.
- This is top-secret classified information which, if disclosed, might alert the target nation, lead to the death of some of the invading troops and/or even cause the invasion to fail.
- The president of the United States, heeding both human and "national technical" intelligence reports, believes the target nation is a base for terrorist activity that probably will be directed against the United States.

Should you print or broadcast what you know? What is the responsible thing to do with information you consider irrefutable?

The answer to both questions is that you should get the story into print or on the air as fast as possible, withholding only the specific day and hour for which the invasion is planned.

Now let's change the scenario in one significant detail: The invasion is *not* scheduled for two weeks in the future. It's to begin so soon that the invading armada already is on the way to the target beaches, and you'll barely have time to get a story in your next edition or broadcast.

In that case, you should refrain from printing or broadcasting the story.

* * *

What's the difference between these two situations? In either case, making the story public will expose classified information, violate national security restrictions and perhaps endanger the national interest. But there's still a considerable difference.

If a story is printed or aired about a military action that is not to take place for two weeks, the exposure of the secret, even with the day and hour withheld, serves to inform the public. It might bring about sufficient public reaction either to force cancellation of the invasion or to give it public sanction. In any event, the story would be informing the public about the plan, which is a prime function of the press.

If the invasion is to start right away, however — tonight or tomorrow morning — the exposure cannot have any such effect on public opinion, and the invasion will go ahead no matter how the public feels about it. Moreover, at that late hour, the story probably would alert the target nation's defenses and could be at least partially responsible for the combat deaths of numerous people, including Americans. The story might even contribute to an American military defeat.

Many persons, including some journalists, would make a strong argument against printing or broadcasting such a story in either of these instances. Information, they'd point out, is classified for a purpose — to protect secrets. Surely the government, in representing all Americans, should be able, in the national interest, to keep at least some secrets, particularly military ones.

Besides, shouldn't the judgment of a president elected by the people and served by elite intelligence agencies be superior to that of a lone reporter and his or her editors, elected by no one? Finally, if the president has made a decision and the military already is carrying it out, isn't it the patriotic duty of the press to be responsible and support — or at least not frustrate — the government's view of what the national interest requires?

Assuming the first case — an invasion starting in two weeks — the argument against publication can be answered point by point.

It is certainly true that classified information is supposed to protect secrets. But what Americans don't usually realize is that almost any federal officeholder, for almost any reason, can be and often is authorized to classify information. Indeed, sometimes the lowest level of officialdom can relegate information to the highest level of secrecy. The judgment of an official thus empowered may be no better, and often is not better, than that of an informed citizen — and not even as good as that of an experienced journalist. Nor is an official's judgment always as dispassionate or disinterested.

The power of classifying almost any information by almost any official has several unfortunate results for the public:

- It bloats the self-importance of many government functionaries out of all proportion to their worth.
- Immense volumes, actual warehouses full, of classified information are kept by the federal government, at astronomical storage costs. Obviously, not all of this classified paper concerns vital diplomatic or military secrets. (Studies have shown, in fact, that routine correspondence and even newspaper clippings are frequently classified.)
- Egregious government abuses often are shielded from public view by the classification — bluntly speaking, the *hiding* — of information not about vital government secrets but about the venality, mistakes, greed or ineptitude — sometimes crimes — of officials and agencies from the White House on down.

Reporters, therefore, have long known that a generalized deference to all classified information is unwarranted and often insupportable. And contrary to widespread opinion, classification is authorized not by legislation but by executive order; it's not a criminal act to disclose such information.

As for those supposedly elite intelligence agencies advising the president, Americans have come to learn that "intelligence" — despite the mystical aura with which its practitioners like to surround the notion and even when gathered by wizard "national technological means" (satellites) — is not necessarily accurate, or timely, or sufficiently verified or gathered by infallible geniuses. Just in recent years, Americans have seen numerous flaws in U.S. intelligence operations: unpredicted nuclear tests in India and Pakistan, the unwarranted U.S. bombing of the Chinese embassy in Belgrade, and the spectacle of a former CIA director being investigated for having transferred classified information to his private home computer.

The hard fact is that decisions based on intelligence information can be no better than the information itself. As with the data fed to computers, GIGO (garbage in, garbage out). Nor are presidential decisions, deserving of respect as they are, necessarily to be regarded as if they were among the Ten Commandments. In lessons learned from Vietnam to Kosovo, the current generation of Americans has seen that decisions of presidents taken in secrecy and based on intelligence can be mistaken, short-sighted and premature, or can go unexpectedly wrong. Sometimes such decisions may even backfire against the national interest. Neither presidents nor intelligence agencies are infallible; it is only that they like to be so considered. More important, they too are servants of those who elect presidents — not the other way around.

Of course, even experienced reporters are not infallible either. Usually, though, their judgments are not swayed by personal or partisan political considerations. And some journalists have been steeped for many years in the issues involved in any president's decisions — more so, sometimes, than he. Furthermore, most are committed to an ethic of informing the public about the public's business, an attitude not always shared by public officials who think they have good reason to operate in secret, shielded from the public's view.

Taken in the round, journalistic decisions about the public interest can be and sometimes are as solid as that of a politically committed, self-interested government official.

The sensational story about the invasion, however, in the preceding hypothetical example concerns a real national-security secret, properly classified. The intelligence on which the president based his order may have been impeccable. No good reporter should disclose such a story lightly, or without high purpose; nor should a reputable newspaper or broadcaster carry it to the public without a similarly defensible motive.

What might such a motive be? To embarrass the president? That is hardly a high purpose. To bring about an American military defeat? Aside from more serious implications, that would be a public-relations disaster for the press. To stop the planned invasion? That might or might not be a high purpose, but it certainly would be a *political* purpose. It would undoubtedly lead to a heated postpublication debate in which the president, the military and the government would likely prevail in the public mind over an "irresponsible" press.

No, for a journalist the high purpose in making the invasion plan public could only be to lay a unilateral decision of the president before the people of a democracy. Such a public revelation gives the people the opportunity either to object to or endorse a military action taken in their name against another nation, with not altogether foreseeable diplomatic and political consequences. It also enables them to pass political judgment on an action in which the lives of fellow Americans — perhaps fathers, brothers or sons — would be put at risk. And in which American *interests* might suffer, too.

It is still disputed in Washington, for example, whether the cruise-missile attack on a purported biological weapons factory in the Sudan in 1999 was predicated on flawed intelligence. Even if the evidence was sufficiently conclusive, some observers question whether President Clinton's order for the missile attack was a proper response. Might it not, critics asked with a certain cynical plausibility, really have been designed to distract public attention from the contemporary Monica Lewinsky scandal and Clinton's impeachment? I doubt that motivation; but Americans may be sure that many persons in the Third World, particularly in the Middle East, questioned the necessity for the attack.

Of course, presidents, as commanders in chief, as custodians of the national interest, as the highest-level consumers of the best-available intelligence information, and presumably as honest persons, rate considerable respect for their national-security decisions. "If you knew what I know," the implicit attitude of presidents freshly briefed by their intelligence gurus, "you'd know I'm doing the right thing." And sometimes they are.

No matter what presidents may wish, however, they do not deserve, nor should they have, the blind obedience of Americans, including journalists. If presidents could command such obedience, they would be more nearly dictators than they already are in foreign and military policy. And if Americans, particularly journalists, did accord presidents such fealty, they would be something less than the free and independent citizens they proudly claim to be. Robust and uninhibited discussion by the people is covered by the First Amendment's guarantees of freedom of the press, assembly and speech, and protected — so far — by the courts. We have no reason or obligation to yield that discussion to presidential decree.

There would be ample reason, therefore, for a reporter to go ahead with the story of an invasion planned for two weeks in the future, particularly if the details could be documented or credible sources identified. If the story had to be based on unidentified sources only, however, no matter how much reason the reporter might have to trust them, the case for publishing would be less clear. Without documented sources, the credibility of the story would be much more open to question by readers and viewers.

As noted earlier, even with the planned invasion two weeks in the future, its actual day and hour should be withheld because so specific an alert should not be given to an adversary. And such specifics are less important to the American public than a general notice of the invasion plan.

On the other hand, if the invasion fleet already is on the move and about to attack, no good rationale exists for making the story public. There's no time for public debate, so the invasion could not be stopped by popular dissent even if strong opposition surfaced. Consequently, publishing the story might only result in death and/or defeat for American forces. Secondarily, the story might result in severe criticism of an "irresponsible" press.

The best that could be accomplished under this second hypothetical scenario would be a comprehensive backgrounder published *after* the invasion. Such a story could discuss how and why the invasion was staged, who favored it and who opposed. Such an article probably would set off vigorous debate as to whether the president's decision had been justified. The piece would not directly serve the press's function as a watchdog for the public interest, but it would still provide a useful service, particularly for similar occasions in the future, that the print press is peculiarly qualified to perform.

The hypothetical invasion could best and most effectively be covered by television, with its remarkable capacity to reach the farthest corners of the world and to relay events via satellite while they are occurring.

Under either scenario, printing or broadcasting the story of the planned invasion *in advance* would be cited by many critics as an example of press irresponsibility. The press would be accused of "blowing" classified national-security information and of contradicting the president's national-security decision.

Journalists should insist, on the other hand, that such a disclosure — certainly if made public two weeks ahead of time — classically served the public's right to know. But to know what? Anything? Everything?

The late syndicated columnist Carl Rowan used to insist, while serving briefly in the sixties as the State Department spokesman, that there was also a public right "*not* to know." He was speaking of certain secrets that if made public certainly would damage the national (that is, the public) interest.

A good example of the right not to know was one of the great secrets of World War II: that the United States had broken an important Japanese code. The resulting intercepts led, most notably, to the vital American naval victory at Midway Island in 1942. After its defeat there, Japan had almost no chance to win the war. Later, the intercepts disclosed that Tokyo was arranging for powerful, suicidal resistance to a planned U.S. invasion of the home islands. Consequently, even without the atomic bomb, the invasion — Operation Olympic — probably would have been canceled.[1] Had the American public been informed of the code breakage, the Japanese would have learned of it, too. They then would have changed the code, thus depriving American forces of an important secret weapon that they were able to use throughout the war.

Few such vital secrets exist, however, particularly in peacetime. Most secrets, if blown, would mean little to the American public or to an adversary. During the Cold War, for example, the geographical specification of American missile targets in the Soviet Union was a closely held top secret. It was enough for Americans to know generally that their missiles were targeted on threatening military sites. Of course, the Soviets could figure out for themselves the likely targets and take steps to guard them. Publication of such a secret, therefore, would have done neither side much good — or harm.

If there's no public right to know *everything,* however, what *does* the public have a right to know? The shortest but most comprehensive answer may be that the public has a right to know what's being done with its tax money and with the authority its votes have conferred on government and its officials. In Cold War times, Americans had a right to know that the military used their tax revenues to aim missiles at important Soviet targets. But Americans did not have a right to know the precise location of those targets, which would have meant little to anyone but an expert on Soviet geography.

The American public clearly would have had a right — even if some citizens didn't particularly want — to know *in advance* about that hypothetical invasion two weeks in the future, planned to be carried out in its name and financed with its tax money. The public would *not* have had so clear a right to know about a military movement scheduled to happen very soon. For reasons I have already mentioned, the public's

---

[1] Richard Frank, *Downfall, the End of the Imperial Japanese Empire* (New York: Random House, 1999), Ch. 13.

right to know is much weaker in this latter instance: There would be no time for public discussion or dissent, and disclosure of the invasion might cause additional deaths and perhaps even military defeat.

The right to know is an important but widely misunderstood and disputed concept, even by journalists. I've occasionally met with groups of young, perhaps even some experienced, reporters and asked the deliberate question: "Would you be willing to commit a crime in order to serve the public's right to know?"

A number of hands immediately go up, followed by impressively bold statements:

> *Sure, I'd be willing to commit a break-in to obtain documents the public needs to know about . . . steal papers off somebody's desk if they proved a public official took a bribe . . . trespass . . . or incite a riot . . . or even endanger life . . . in pursuit of the people's right to know . . .*

I then ask the follow-up question: "If you did any of those things, would you be willing to go to jail as a consequence?"

The hands quickly go down and plaintive cries arise:

> *Why should I go to jail for serving the public's right to know?*

Because, I reply, the right to know is not a legal concept. It is not specified in the Constitution, it is not embodied in law, and it is certainly not a valid defense in court. A reporter may feel morally or ethically justified in breaking the law in order to inform the public about something he or she thinks the public has a right to know. But that reporter has committed a crime for which a jail sentence may have to be served.

It never ceases to amaze me how many reporters don't know, or refuse to believe, the simple fact that journalists have no right to commit a crime even when they believe they're acting in the public interest. Some reporters, in fact, do commit crimes they believe are justified. Such reporters may be ignorant of their legal culpability or, in rare instances, willing to accept the legal consequences in order to serve that abstraction in which they so strongly believe — the public's right to know.

I, too, believe in that right, as defined previously. And I, too, am willing to challenge power, defy opinion, risk opprobrium, anger my peers and confound accepted "truths" (there's an undeniable satisfaction in all of that) in order to inform the public of what I believe it has a right to know. I am *not* willing, though, and I think journalists seldom should be willing, to commit a crime to further what is a conceptual — not a constitutional — right.

This raises the question of "civil disobedience" — that useful procedure in which citizens openly and knowingly defy a law in order to challenge it in court, or at least before public opinion. Perhaps the best-known and most successful civil disobedience in modern times was that of black youths in the South during the 1950s and 1960s who courageously mounted sit-ins at lunch counters and other places from which segregationist laws previously had barred them. The sit-ins forced the repeal of those unjust laws, and properly so.

Those who engaged in them, however, were prepared to take the consequences — physical abuse as well as jail. In fact, most knew that jail was a likely penalty, and often it was. They sat in anyway and should be honored for doing so.

What about journalists, then, who break the law in order to challenge it? If that is truly the motive, their actions may well be justified. But in such cases, the issue at stake should be a more specific one of justice and equality rather than the merely conceptual right to know. Laws against theft and break-ins are not always unjust in the way that lunch-counter segregation obviously was.

A reporter, black or white, who deliberately joined a 1950s sit-in as an act of overt civil disobedience would have been justified. But a reporter who breaks into someone's office in order to steal a document incriminating a bigoted official should be subject to criminal law. This holds true even if the reporter believes that he or she is acting ethically for a good cause and is fully aware of the possible consequences.

How far a journalist should legally go in upholding the public's right to know, therefore, is often a matter of individual conscience. Should reporters break the law and take the consequences, or should they follow a different course of action? Either way, reporters should consider the right to know, though not in the Constitution, to be vital to citizenship in a democracy. Obviously, if the public doesn't know what's about to happen, could happen or may already be happening, it can have no informed opinion and cannot exercise an informed citizen's duty to agree or dissent.

That seems to me an unarguable proposition concerning *public* activities — that is, those sponsored by government and paid for by tax revenues. Even Congress has slowly and reluctantly come to the view that the public does have a right to know, and therefore the press has a right to report, what goes on in congressional committee meetings. That is where most significant legislative action occurs, and most of them, not too long ago, were tightly closed to press and public.

The public's right to know is less clear, however — it's often strenuously denied — in the realm of *private* activities, no matter how important to the public. Put simply, the public surely has a right to know what an elected town council is doing or about to do with town funds. But does the same public have a right to know what an important local industry is doing that may have a profound effect on the townspeople and others? The management of that industry might well deny, and usually does, the right to know; a lot of Americans, even some of those affected, might well agree.

I once remarked to the publisher of *The New York Times* that I thought we were delinquent in not sufficiently reporting the inner workings of major corporations, some of which rivaled Congress in their effect on the public. If we thought it a duty to report on Congress, why shouldn't we also send reporters to cover corporate board meetings? And to set a good example, why not assign a *Times* reporter to cover the next board of directors meeting of *The New York Times*?

"Over my dead body," replied the man who had approved publication of the Pentagon Papers. That was the end of that, as it would have been, and is, throughout the American press.

Private business is private in the corporate view, and this attitude is shared by the press, which is, after all, a business itself. The public can find out about businesses, if at all — whether the development of a new model automobile or the pollution of a river or the desecration of a forest — from favorably timed and produced public relations efforts or as a result of some fait accompli, like a mountainside already lost to strip mining.

Environmental and consumer consciousness and resulting legislation have modified the defiant corporate view to a considerable extent. Generally speaking, however, the American press still does not report on the plans and workings of American corporations except as those corporations themselves choose to disclose selected, usually self-serving, information; or if a prosecution or a lawsuit forces a less-favored method of disclosure, as in the case of the government's antitrust suit against the mammoth Microsoft Corporation. For practical purposes, then, the public's right to know applies only to *public* institutions and activities. There is no right to know who a movie or rock star is sleeping with, no matter how interesting the story may be. There probably *is* a right to know about a married U.S. senator's bed partner if it's not his or her spouse, but that brings up the right-to-privacy issue that is discussed in Chapter 3.

In recent years, the most controversial and decisive pursuit of the public's right to know was the publication in 1971 by *The New York Times,* and ultimately by others, of the so-called Pentagon Papers.

The Papers, as noted earlier, were a collection of documents compiled in the Pentagon at the direction of Robert S. McNamara, who was secretary of defense in the Kennedy and part of the Johnson administrations. The Papers outlined the origins of and U.S. rationale for the war in Vietnam. They were classified top secret and had remained undisclosed to the public during the first years of the Nixon administration.

Heavily influenced by his national security adviser, Henry Kissinger, President Nixon came to believe that publication of the Papers endangered the government's ability to keep secrets; he also was angered by the *Times'* defiance of the principle of classification. His administration soon asked for and got a federal injunction against further publication.

Not prepared to defy a specific court order, the *Times* ceased publication but fought the issue all the way to the Supreme Court. So did *The Washington Post,* which had obtained the Papers and started publishing them soon after the *Times.* The court expedited its proceedings and after a few days, amid intense public controversy, ruled that the injunction was an unconstitutional "prior restraint." Therefore, the *Times* and the *Post* could and did resume publication. Other newspapers followed suit.

The episode was important not only in increasing public resistance to the war in Vietnam but in clarifying the meaning of the First Amendment. In particular, it confirmed the government's lack of power to prevent the press *in advance* from publishing a story. That's what is meant by "prior restraint."

The publication of the Pentagon Papers and the reaction to the Supreme Court ruling demonstrated, however, the essential ambivalence of American public opinion about a free press. While the *Times* was enjoined by the government from publishing, those named in the federal injunction — including me, I'm proud to say — often met in

New York to discuss developments. One night, we all went out to dinner at Christ Cella, then a well-known steak house (lamentably closed now). As our group (identified by badges that proclaimed "Free The New York Times 21") entered, other restaurant patrons stood and applauded — a cherished moment I doubt I'll ever experience again.

By that and other measures of opinion, we were confident that the public was in favor of the *Times* in its struggle against an overpowering government. Once the court ruled, however, and publication resumed, public opinion seemed to swing massively the other way. Even the government, people seemed to be saying, can't restrain *The New York Times* and the arrogant American press.

To this day, I believe most Americans have mixed feelings about a free press. They fear and resist government control of the press, but they also fear and resist the exaggerated idea that no one can limit the power of the press.[2]

---

[2] See Chapter 10 for further discussion of this duality.

CHAPTER 5

Deep Throat*

For the Christmas holidays of 1962, President Kennedy and his entourage went, as they often did, to Palm Beach, Fla. The White House press corps went as well, and at that time I was the White House correspondent for *The New York Times.* Being away from home and family at Christmas — a plight to which White House reporters become inured — was at least partially compensated by two weeks in sunny Florida. Not a few reporters put in a lot of the time on the golf links or the tennis court.

On one of the last days of the year, however, the White House press had to earn its keep. Pierre Salinger, the presidential press secretary, announced that the president would meet with reporters to review the events of the year 1962. That afternoon, 20 or 30 reporters — some disgruntled at playtime cut short — piled into a bus chartered to take them to the holiday White House (not the Kennedy family house but one next door, which apparently was considered more suitable as presidential quarters).

We gathered in a big sunny parlor overlooking the beach and the Atlantic Ocean, most of us sitting on the floor or leaning against the walls. Some did a little sub-rosa spying on the first family's private residence. I was interested, for example, to note that a Chubby Checker disc was on the record player; the Twist then was at its height of popularity.

Salinger soon announced the ground rules of the meeting. Publication, for one thing, was proscribed until a certain "release date." That was expected and accepted by all since it would prevent any one person from rushing into print or on the air ahead of everyone else. On

---

* *Washington Post* reporters Bob Woodward and Carl Bernstein gave this name to their famous anonymous source in the Watergate case of the 1970s. The source is *still* unidentified.

the other hand, if any sensational news were disclosed, the release date meant that the press would have to keep it secret for a certain period despite the public's right to know.

Salinger's ground rules permitted us to use our own words in reporting whatever Kennedy told us, but we could not use direct quotations or write that Kennedy himself had been the source of our information. For attribution, we were to use the ridiculous formula that everything in our stories actually had been learned from unnamed "friends of the president."

Readers were supposed to believe that the White House press, either singly or in a body, had sought out certain friends of the president who then had told us what President Kennedy thought about the year just past. Or, even less likely, readers could infer that those well-informed or super-intuitive friends had sought *us* out in order to leak Kennedy's views on such happenings as the contested and bloody integration of the University of Mississippi.

Some friends these would be, not only to know Kennedy's private thoughts but to be willing to spill them to the press!

Nevertheless, that was the rule and it had precedent, which was a weighty factor in Washington journalism and politics. This was to be a backgrounder, one of the established rituals of the arcane relationship between officials and reporters in the nation's capital. (This kind of backgrounder is not to be confused with the kind of soft-news retrospective article discussed in Chapter 2.) A backgrounder of the sort held at Palm Beach is an official's news conference with a group of reporters or an interview with a single reporter — but with the crucial added requirement that the person holding the news conference or giving the interview may not be identified by name or specific position.

The "friends of the president" dodge was unusual, if not unique. At most backgrounders, a more plausible identification of the source is permitted, such as "a government official," "a highly placed official," "an official well informed about the decision" or that familiar old chestnut "an informed source." Occasionally, an ingenious reporter may work in additional information, such as "a source bitterly opposed to the policy" or "a knowledgeable member of Congress with no love for the administration." Direct quotations can be attributed to such ghostly personages.

No matter how qualified or how vulnerable to an outsider's guesswork, a backgrounder always gives those holding it a degree of anonymity. Many reasons may be adduced for high-level unwillingness to be named, although those who hold backgrounders ordinarily would be hungry for publicity. The speaker may be floating a trial balloon, trying to gauge public reaction without being linked to the balloon. He or she may be stating a controversial policy or decision still being debated within the government. No official speaker will willingly take responsibility for saying something that might give offense to a foreign nation or to an important domestic political faction. And if a policy being outlined should later fail or have to be reversed, the speaker would not be publicly identified with it. Some undertakings, moreover, are so experimental or controversial that it's not unreasonable for an administration — let alone a single official — not to be too publicly or officially committed to it. And all officials and administrations seek to operate as much as possible in secrecy; it's the nature of the game to try to avoid the pressures of public opinion, pro or particularly con.

Sometimes there's a special reason for demanding anonymity. If a particular decision or policy, for instance, could be traced to a particular official or agency, its political chances might be damaged. Or if, say, the Department of Defense knew that the Department of State was taking a particular line, bitter internecine warfare might erupt. Governments are not much different from families in their internal rivalries. Finally, there are occasions when the backgrounder is mostly an effort to avoid any responsibility at all or to denounce someone surreptitiously: "A highly placed source said today that Senator Goosebump had cast his vote under the influence of the dairy lobby."

In all such cases, the press is complicitous in the degree of anonymity it allows the speaker. This anomaly in a press loudly boastful of its dedication to the public's right to know can be simply explained: The press wants the information offered in a backgrounder badly enough to be willing to grant the anonymity. Does the press want to pass the information on to the public? Of course it does, but it also wants to satisfy its own insider's yearning to be "in the know." The backgrounder — in Washington or anywhere — is a major reason why the press often knows more than it tells the public.

At the Palm Beach backgrounder in 1962, President Kennedy insisted on being nameless for a number of reasons. He could discuss both foreign and domestic events and some of the personalities involved in both without being held diplomatically, politically or personally responsible for the views he might express. He knew that some persons he might explicitly or implicitly criticize — Chairman Nikita

Khrushchev of the Soviet Union or the "Wizard of Ooze," as wags called Republican Senator Everett McKinley Dirksen, the minority leader — were in a position to retaliate. Nor did Kennedy want to tip his official hand about future policies and decisions.

Besides, every word a president speaks — if he's known to have spoken it — will be pored over at home and abroad for supposedly hidden meanings and nuances. From some of these, far-fetched notions (as well as a few plausible conclusions) might well be drawn.

Beyond all that, like the proverbial 800-pound gorilla who can sit where he wants, a president is powerful and important enough to set any ground rules he pleases. If a lower-level official seeks anonymity for disclosing something less than earthshaking, the press might simply ignore the proffered information or demand that it be put "on the record." That's not likely to happen to a president.

Reporters, and presumably the public, are so eager to learn what the chief executive believes or wants or plans that almost any terms he sets will be accepted. The television networks are heavily criticized, for instance, when they refuse to clear time for a presidential speech, even when they have a valid reason for the refusal.

No reporter at Kennedy's holiday White House — including me — protested the ground rules Salinger laid down. We were aware of the reasons and precedents that more or less validated presidential anonymity, no matter how transparent. Nor did anyone want publicly to break ranks with other reporters, our colleagues and peers. The solidarity of the pack is as strong in jounalism as elsewhere. Mostly, however, we wanted Kennedy's views and expected them to make a good story.

In any case, Kennedy soon entered the room, and that settled the matter. As it turned out, those "friends of the president" knew quite a lot about what he was thinking, past, present and for the future. One thing they knew was that the president thought it necessary in the coming year, 1963, to be more forceful with U.S. allies like Britain and West Germany. The president wanted American views to weigh more heavily within allied councils than he thought they had in the past.

This did not seem like particularly sensational news to me. It did not refer to any specific point, nor was it phrased as a threat. Consequently, in my story I reported this remark fairly far down in a lengthy article that led the *Times* front page. As I recall, most of my colleagues played it down too, with the startling exception of Frank Cormier, the White House reporter for the Associated Press. Ordinarily, as the representative of numerous newspapers and broadcasters of all political persuasions, the AP was cautious, nearly neutral, in its leads and wording. And the late Frank Cormier himself was neither an excitable nor an ideological reporter. He was careful and conscientious, after considerable experience in Washington journalism.

On this occasion, however, Cormier rather inexplicably led his article for the AP with Kennedy's intent to be more forceful with the allies. In the opinion of the White House and of other reporters, such treatment gave Kennedy's words more importance than they warranted. A London newspaper further amplified — or distorted — their significance with a scare headline over the AP story that read something like this:

KENNEDY: I'LL DECIDE

Coupled with such headlines, Cormier's lead brought about virtually an international incident. This was a graphic example of the power of the press and of one reporter's understanding of a particular remark. The reaction was so alarming to the administration, which was anxious to stay on good terms with its allies, that it tried to squelch the interpretation of the president's words represented by the London headline.

To do so, Salinger produced a White House transcript from a supposedly anonymous backgrounder! This transcript not only provided the exact text of Kennedy's words but left no doubt whatsoever that *he* had spoken them — not those ubiquitous "friends" supposedly privy to his thoughts.

Worse, to counter the London headline and other damaging effects of Cormier's article, which had been widely printed by AP clients abroad, Salinger made the transcript available only to *foreign* correspondents in Washington, just a few of whom had been invited to the Palm Beach backgrounder. Naturally, this apparent favoritism evoked the rage of American reporters like me. We had abided by the Palm Beach rules and written the story only from our own notes, without direct quotations and in the absurd "friends" formula. Now we found that a transcript of Kennedy's exact words, attributed directly to him, was being handed out to foreign correspondents, most of whom had not even been present at the backgrounder. People around the world actually were being given knowledge denied to American readers and viewers.

To calm matters, Salinger then offered the transcript to American reporters too. The obvious effect, however, was that the president's backgrounder was blown completely, and the "friends of the president" formula was shown to be a flat-out lie. It became clear to many citizens that the lie first had been propounded by the White House and then adopted and advanced by a compliant press in abject dismissal of Americans' supposed right to know. Oh, what a tangled web we weave, it has been well said, when first we practice to deceive.

The denouement of this episode did not develop quickly enough, unfortunately, for me. When my story had appeared, detailing what "friends of the president" had to say about his inner thoughts, an interested reader was my august senior colleague Arthur Krock. (Formerly the *Times* Washington bureau chief, Mr. Krock at that time was the author of a thrice-weekly editorial-page column, "In the Nation," to the authorship of which I later succeeded.) Deeply versed in the ways of the capital, Mr. Krock[1] was not taken in by the "friends of the president" nonsense and therefore wrote a column based on the presidential views described in my news report. Mr. Krock flatly stated, however, that such views could have come from no one but John F. Kennedy himself.

Quite honorably, Mr. Krock had never asked me to disclose the identity of the source; rather, he drew an obvious conclusion. Since he had not been present at the Palm Beach backgrounder, moreover, he did not consider himself bound by the rules Salinger had set, and he wasn't.

Administration officials, including Salinger, took the immediate position, however, that I must have told Mr. Krock that the president himself had spoken directly, though not for quotation, to the press. Had I done so, I would have been in severe violation of the backgrounder's rules and subject to the opprobrium of my colleagues. Copious denials on my part and Mr. Krock's dignified assertion of his and my innocence convinced neither the White House nor some other reporters. Fortunately, the flap over Cormier's article soon obscured my supposed transgression, although I always felt thereafter that I had been at least faintly compromised in Pierre Salinger's eyes.

Nearly 40 years later, all this may seem the proverbial tempest in a teapot. What is important is that such foul-ups no doubt continue within the Washington press. The Palm Beach backgrounder and the

---

[1] No one who worked with him would have dreamed of calling him anything but "Mr. Krock."

controversies it caused aptly illustrate some of the enduring complexities of journalism. Not the least of these is the constant problem of how to justify printing or broadcasting a particular piece of information, or whether it *can* be justified.

Suppose the governor of your state promised in his or her election campaign never — no, never — to seek a tax increase ("read my lips"). Now, a year later, you're writing a story revealing that the governor is about to seek a tax increase after all. (In the trade, your article would be known as a *dope story* because it supposedly gives the reader inside dope not officially acknowledged.)

In preparing such a story, you should ask yourself a number of questions about your sources:

- How many sources of information for this sensational story should I have?
- Should these sources be named?
- If the governor is not one of them, how did the sources learn what they profess to know?
- Are their motives favorable or hostile to the governor? To a tax increase?
- Do any of the sources stand to profit, financially or politically, from the story I'm writing?
- Is my article likely to change the governor's mind?
- Could my story make it impossible for the governor to retreat from the proposed tax increase?
- Is the story a fair presentation of the governor's intention?

Sourcing, in other words, is a major consideration in substantial news accounts, although a problem with sources usually doesn't arise except in dope stories. For instance, if a senator speaks in the legislature, a candidate takes a poll and publishes the results, the police report an accident, a house burns, or a mayor makes available the text of her inaugural remarks, there is no question involving sourcing. The source is obvious and undisputed because it is based on an open announcement or a recorded act, and only the details of the story need concern the reporter and his or her editors.

In any number of other cases, though, such as Kennedy's Palm Beach backgrounder, the source of the alleged information is all important. If a source can't be trusted by the public, is obviously biased one way or the other or isn't even known, how can the story be taken seriously?

If your story can assert, however, that the governor's chief of staff said the governor was going to demand a tax increase, few readers or viewers will doubt it. Better still, if the governor himself will fess up, the story obviously is true (and it's no longer a dope story).

If, on the other hand, merely "informed" but unnamed sources make the allegation in your story, and if the governor then does not act as predicted, the public may well conclude that the story was an example of press malice or irresponsibility. In fact, even if the governor does nothing, the story that he would seek a tax increase may have been true *when written* — but so poorly or unwisely attributed as to leave the governor room ("wiggle room," in the vernacular) to retreat without appearing to have done so. A dope story of that magnitude, in fact, may be so badly received by the public that the governor would indeed change his mind.

To avoid such pitfalls, a reporter customarily should have at least two reliable *identified* sources for a controversial story like this. Otherwise, even if the story was true when written, it will be vulnerable to a political reversal and denial by the person involved, in this case the governor.

If, however, your sources are reliable but refuse to be identified, you'll have to make a value judgment — a not uncommon requirement of journalism. Should you go ahead with an important story even though it may be denied and appear to have been untrue? If you do go ahead, trusting your unnamed sources, it's doubly important to have at least two of them. Just as patients often like to have a second doctor's opinion before submitting to surgery, readers or viewers are reassured if a story claims that the information was confirmed or verified by a second, even unidentified, source.

Nevertheless, for a story as provocative as a governor getting ready to undo a serious campaign pledge, it would be far safer and far more credible if an obviously well-informed source, such as the governor's chief of staff, could be quoted. But suppose the chief of staff *is* the source and refuses to be identified on the grounds that she'd be fired if her name were used?

That alone should sharpen the reporter's suspicion — which his professional skepticism should already have aroused — that this high-level leak is in fact only a trial balloon. If the public reaction is hostile enough, neither the governor nor his staff chief will be publicly committed to the alleged tax increase and probably nothing more will be heard of it. The reporter and the press, however, will be stuck with a story that misled the public and gave both a heightened reputation for irresponsibility or worse.

Therefore, even with the chief of staff's apparent leak in hand, the reporter must seek out a second source. One way to do this, crafty but often effective, would be to approach another high-level official — perhaps the state director of taxation — and casually ask if the director thinks the governor's plan for a tax increase is justified. If the director denies the existence of any such plan, another caution flag will have gone up. But if the director is willing to discuss it — which is possible since the reporter apparently knows about it anyway — that's confirmation enough.

Assuming such a bluff works, the reporter then can write the tax-increase story with a certain confidence, even without identified sources. It might read something like this:

> Contradicting his own campaign pledge, Governor Bullhead plans to make the case for a substantial tax increase in a television address next Wednesday. Two of his highest-level appointees, both of whom declined to be identified, have provided *The Daily Bugle* with details of the governor's tax plan.

Two "highest-level appointees" providing "details," which of course would be discussed later in the story, constitute a fairly solid guarantee of its credibility. Pegging the TV address to "next Wednesday" (which is what Henry James called the "solidity of specification") helps as well. Moreover, this kind of attribution pretty strongly commits Governor Bullhead. At the very least, if he now backs off, he'll have a hard time explaining himself to his own colleagues and to those who've presumably been pressuring him for a tax increase.

Writing only that the governor "plans" to — not "will" — make the speech also gives the reporter a little wiggle room. Any journalist knows that when a politician says he or she plans or has no plans to do something, it doesn't mean they will or won't do it; rather, it often means nothing.

In this case, a strong follow-up article is virtually demanded. Such an article will make it even harder for Bullhead to back off, if he's so inclined. Once the original story gets wide circulation, more sources are likely to come forward to confirm the governor's plan. They'll be anxious for the public to think that they were "in the know" as part of the Bullhead inner circle, even if they weren't.

In a slightly different scenario, however, suppose that the governor's plan is such a closely guarded secret that no confirmation of the chief of staff's leak can be had. Should the reporter still go ahead with the story? Although a chief of staff is certainly in a position to know the governor's intention, what is the motive for such a portentous leak? Is the staff chief perhaps trying to shoot down the tax plan before the governor can throw his political weight behind it? Is she trying to expose a planned flip-flop in the hope of preventing it? Might the chief be trying to force Bullhead's hand before antitax elements push the governor the other way? Is it possible there's no such tax-increase plan and the chief of staff is trying to embarrass the governor by suggesting that there is? If so, why? Is the chief perhaps in some trouble with the governor? Does she have future political plans that Bullhead's embarrassment might further?

The reporter should do his or her best to answer these questions as part of the needed value judgment, and personal expertise and experience are perhaps the most reliable guides. In fact, any of these questions might lead to a better story than the original dope piece, such as an article on dissension in the governor's office, political betrayal or a high-level struggle for Bullhead's favor. At the least, these questions should lead the reporter to *qualify* as fully as possible the identification of the high-level appointee. For instance:

> This high-level appointee, *considered in political circles to be a potential rival of the governor,* explained that . . .

Or:

> This well-known appointee, *believed to be pushing the governor in a more liberal direction,* suggested . . .

Such qualifications still preserve the agreed-upon anonymity of the source, but they help an outsider judge the value and meaning of the story. Even when there are two or more unnamed sources, qualifications like these are often important. A reporter needs to personally evaluate each source. Are the source's motives impersonal? Has the reporter experienced this source's trustworthiness? Does the source's information fit with whatever else the reporter may know about the situation and the personalities involved?

Over the years, I have written a few news stories based entirely on the word of one unidentified source. In no such case was I disappointed or betrayed in my confidence. But in each instance, because I had a long and deep experience of that source's integrity, I was willing to trust the source at the risk of my own credibility. I would not advise other reporters to follow that course except in the rare case where they may have, as I did, complete and experienced faith in that particular source. Most of the time, using two or more sources — either named or unidentified — is not only better but just plain common sense.

Nonjournalists may well ask, however, "Why use unidentified sources at all?"

In fact, numerous surveys of news consumers suggest that frequent attributions of important information to unnamed persons are one of the main causes of the public's distrust of journalism — a distrust as strong, unfortunately, as is the public's jaundiced view of politicians.

This distrust is the major problem with unidentified sources: Their use diminishes confidence in any story that relies on them and diminishes confidence in the press generally. Furthermore, since newspapers and broadcasters are often willing to quote unidentified sources, the practice quickly multiplies. Most politicians and some government officials are sophisticated students of journalism. They see that they can demand anonymity and get it, even when there's no compelling reason except personal or political convenience. It's hard for the press to stand on a principle so often violated or ignored.

A lesser but real problem with unidentified sources is the temptation for journalists to invent them: in effect, to falsify a story by making up a source or a compelling quotation. That temptation exists anytime the verification of information is difficult to obtain and because no reader or viewer, even the most informed, can tell for sure whether an unnamed source or a quote from such a source is invented or real. Too often, the public assumes the unnamed source must be invented; else, why unidentified?

(When an unidentified source must be used, avoiding the suspicion of falsification is another good reason to qualify as much as possible by saying, for example, "a person involved in the investigation" or "a longtime supporter of the senator." Unhappily, such qualifications can be invented too — and sometimes are.)

Our earlier question persists: Why must an unidentified source
ever be used?

The answer, though unconvincing to many critics, is that sometimes
there's no other way to make necessary information public. Perhaps
someone who has information will lose a job if identified as a leaker or a
whistle-blower. Or perhaps that person won't be nominated or hired.
Releasing certain information may cause votes, or even elections, to be
lost. Some potential sources may fear divorce, ostracism, or other forms
of vengeance. Political influence and power may be at stake. Financial
supporters or public backers of a candidate may believe that if their
identity is disclosed, the information they give will seem biased and lack
the desired effect. For any number of reasons, valid or self-serving, a
source may not agree to be identified in the press.

In every such instance, reporters and editors are obligated, once
again, to make a mature, balanced judgment: Does the information
seem so important — necessary, say, to send an embezzler to jail —
that it should be made known to the public even if it may turn out to be
in error? Is revealing the information worth the risk of a loss of credibility for the press? Or the suspicion of falsifying?

Clearly the risks are great. But sometimes the needed information
does seem that important. In fact, the more significant the information
seems, the more likely the informant will be to demand anonymity —
and the more difficult the journalistic decision. All prices go up with
the apparent value of the goods.

Anonymity obviously should be granted sparingly and only after
intensive inquiry into the motives and reasoning of the source
demanding it. If he or she has no good reason, which is often the case,
every effort should be made to have the information put "on the
record" — for the source to agree to be named. A decision to permit or
deny anonymity is one that reporters frequently have to make, sometimes without even consulting their editors; and readers or viewers
usually know little of the circumstances involved.

Occasionally, if information already has been disclosed to a
reporter but the source can establish no strong reason for anonymity,
the reporter may decide to go ahead and name him or her without per-
mission. Such a drastic step, however, should never be taken after a
reporter has promised not to do it. At that point, the reporter's word
and honor are on the line. Furthermore, no such disclosure should ever
be made unless it's absolutely necessary in order to get desired and

vital information to the public, and then only if the reporter believes the source's refusal to be identified is merely self-serving.

Regrettably, these "rules," which are mostly my own and not those of any official body, are often flouted by reporters or news agencies too eager for a story to concern themselves with credibility or even with their own integrity. Steven Brill, the press critic, recalls hearing a television reporter attribute a story to "a source" on a noon broadcast and then to "sources" on a later broadcast. Brill says he called the reporter to ask how many additional sources had come forward between broadcasts, but he received no satisfactory answer.

Regrettably, too, such official events as Kennedy's Palm Beach backgrounder and those like it at the subpresidential level, elevate — if that's the appropriate word — the use of unidentified or misidentified sources to standard procedure that most often benefits politicians and usually belies the public's right to know.

In the innumerable backgrounders conducted aboard his aircraft by Secretary of State Henry Kissinger during his celebrated "shuttle diplomacy" in the Middle East during the Ford administration, Kissinger permitted reference to himself only as "a high official." At other times, Kissinger was exceptionally adept at keeping significant diplomatic information in his own hands, dispensing it to invited State Department reporters only at regular backgrounders in his office. Reporters whose coverage had in some way displeased Kissinger were not invited to these informative soirees. This policy served the dual purpose of keeping those reporters in the dark about important matters known to their competitors and making them anxious to avoid the secretary's displeasure.

If the public doesn't know and can only guess at a "high official's" identity or position (which was not that difficult during Kissinger's shuttle diplomacy), is the public really served by backgrounder information? The answer is that some backgrounders serve the public well, some moderately, some not at all, and perhaps some actually do a disservice. What they all have in common is that reporters, when confronted with an official or a politician announcing that he or she is speaking only "on background," have little choice but to go along.

Why don't reporters band together and refuse to cover backgrounders, forcing those who conduct them to speak "on the record"? The reason is that newspaper and broadcasting businesses are not cooperatives and do not relish being at a competitive disadvantage. If one or two newspapers or broadcasters tried to organize a boycott of backgrounders, others would recognize the opportunity, refuse to go along, and be able to feature stories — perhaps important stories — that the boycotters would not be able to report. And if several news organizations agreed not to report backgrounders, powerful and plausible charges of conspiracy and collusion by the all-powerful press surely would come from the government and its supporters. Think what the Nixon administration might have done with such an opportunity to wound the press the president hated.

As a rookie reporter in Washington, I attended one of the breakfasts organized by Godfrey Sperling, then a St. Louis correspondent. Sperling staged these "dutch" breakfasts every week or so and invited an important political figure as the guest. The guest might be a Senate committee chairman, a Cabinet member or a national party official. The assembled reporters asked questions and the guest, who was to remain unidentified, answered. Thus reporters got a story and the guest got publicity for whatever he or she might have proposed or opposed.

I should have known that any such occasion would be "on background." But I was a rookie and made a foolish mistake. In my later story, I fully identified that morning's breakfast guest — mercifully, these years later, I've forgotten who it was. I haven't forgotten, however, that Sperling, the guest and the other invited reporters were outraged. Nor was the *Times* pleased that I had so blatantly jeopardized my access to important officials. Ultimately, I wrote each of the other reporters a letter of abject apology — and never again neglected to make sure of the ground rules under which someone was speaking.

Even more problematical for the press is the so-called *deep backgrounder,* at which no reference of any kind may be made to the person imparting the information. Reporters may not even mention that there is such a person. This kind of backgrounder is sometimes called "legal plagiarism" because it calls for a reporter to write what may be a major story entirely on his or her own authority, if any. For instance:

> The United States will withhold diplomatic recognition from the new regime in Lower Slobbovia until the dissidents who overthrew President Hypervent's government agree to permit no hostile military bases on Slobbovian soil.

Not only is there no attribution here, but there is no admission that anyone decided anything, or anyone spoke or anyone listened. The reporter is presumed to have these "facts" out of his or her own knowledge, gained by some unspecified process from some unmentionable source — not even a "high official." The more authoritative the reporter's byline — as, say, Peter Jennings' or Tom Brokaw's is today — and the more the reporter's organization is respected, the more weight even such a baldly unsupported story will have. And, of course, vice versa. This is why deep background is more often provided to a major paper like *The Washington Post* than to the Podunk *Herald.*

Deep background is nevertheless risky for source and press alike. The source risks that the story disclosed will have so little credibility that it will fail to accomplish the desired political, diplomatic or military end. The advantage, at least, is that the story has "deniability," which means the source can deny any responsibility if the story backfires.

The reporter writing such an unsubstantiated story runs a heightened risk that it may not be true or that what's touted may not work out. Or the deep backgrounder may only be floating a trial balloon; it could even be a canny maneuver using the press to achieve some unstated effect.

Deep background paradoxically requires a greater degree of trust on both sides than is usually required of skeptical reporters and scheming officials. The reporter obviously must have considerable confidence in the truth of the information and the integrity of the unmentioned source. The source, on the other hand, and the government organization he or she represents must be reasonably certain that any official involvement will not be made public.

As pointed out earlier, backgrounders and deep backgrounders contribute heavily to a "dirty little secret" of the press: that much of what newspapers and broadcasters know can't be passed on to the public; that in fact the press often collaborates with politicians, officials, businesses, institutions and authority generally rather than exposing its workings to public view.

An experienced reporter will almost always form at least a friendly, sometimes much closer, relationship with someone he or she regularly covers, such as a mayor, a legislator, a company treasurer, a member of a board of trustees, perhaps a Cabinet officer — rarely a president — or more likely a press spokesperson for any of the above.

Those closer relationships can cause much trouble, particularly if between the sexes. But even same-sex friendships can lead to requests for special favors, which are sometimes granted. All too often, a reporter may withhold information that would be potentially harmful to a "friend" who wants it withheld. For that reason, reporters do well to avoid anything more than civil, friendly relations with their sources, even at the sacrifice of greater access — which it usually will be. Admittedly, it's hard to tell when "close" is "too close." I used to tell reporters in the Washington bureau of the *Times,* in tones of weary wisdom, "Be neither in nor out." That's good advice but a hard balance to hit.

Even mere friendship, more often than not, will lead to confidential conversations, sometimes casual and sometimes planned, in which the reporter will learn certain information on condition that he or she not print or broadcast it. Perhaps the mayor plans to serve only one term, or a legislator is going to cast a controversial vote. Such information may be confided to a reporter for a variety of reasons but only rarely by accident. Perhaps it is confided because of genuine friendship, as a virtual "bribe" to gain a reporter's favor on other matters, to force the reporter's silence on something he or she is going to find out anyway, or occasionally to bargain for the timing or the prominence of publication.

In any case, if a reporter accepts information "off the record," particularly if he or she actually has sought such a confidence, the reporter is obligated to abide by the deal no matter how tempting it may be to write or broadcast an exclusive story. Allowing or urging a source to go off the record is so solemn an undertaking that many reporters actually will put away pen and notebook, particularly a tape recorder, to symbolize the obligation.

Reporters have been known, not infrequently, to place themselves in contempt of court and to go to jail to honor an off-the-record obligation. Giving one's word and then keeping it is a matter of a reporter's pride and honor, as it is for most of us. It is also the basis for a profound degree of trust between the press and many public figures. For most reporters, violating an off-the-record agreement, however incautiously or involuntarily made, would be unthinkable. Some states even protect such arrangements with so-called shield laws.

Despite the public's right to know, reporters often seek or accept off-the-record information, and not all of these arrangements deserve scorn. Off-the-record knowledge can fill important gaps in a reporter's knowledge and enable him or her to write other, more informed stories (without violating the off-the-record pledge) than he or she could write otherwise. Sometimes, moreover, the only way to get certain information from a source — at least the reporter believes it's the only way — is to agree to accept it off the record.

Even if that specific knowledge may not be written or broadcast, it may answer other questions in other stories, tell something important about the source or shed light on the political or diplomatic situation. If nothing else, it may improve a reporter's relationship with a source and make the reporter better informed, both of which can be useful on other stories. All reporters need to feel that they understand, even secretly, what's going on; if they do, their stories are likely to be more informative to the public, despite some withheld information.

Holding back some kinds of knowledge, then, may perhaps be all to the good, or so many journalists believe. On the other hand, allowing sources to speak off the record covers up, either temporarily or permanently, information the public may be entitled to know. It frequently serves the self-interest of politicians and other figures, perhaps to the detriment of the public interest. It advances the cause of secrecy, which ought to be journalism's mortal enemy. And it's the antithesis, in most cases, of boastful press claims to serve the public's interest and knowledge. Nor is such collusion with sources of information consonant with the intent of the First Amendment, that glowing pronouncement so jealously guarded and zealously promoted by the press.

Two personal stories may suggest the ambiguity of off-the-record arrangements:

Not long after I'd served as one of the negotiators during the Attica prison riot in 1971, I met with some of the others to plan a future course of action. I was the only reporter in the group.

Our appointed chairman spoke first: "Of course, this meeting will be off the record."

I immediately stood up and replied, perhaps a little self-righteously: "Then I can't take part."

So I left. Within hours after the meeting, one of the other participants gave me "a fill," as reporters say, on what had been decided, which was very little. That illustrated a lesson I already knew: A reporter doesn't have to accept off-the-record information. Usually, it can be learned some other way.

On a quite different occasion — a posh private luncheon in Washington — a number of high officials, including Vice President Hubert H. Humphrey, were at the table. The talk, including a good deal of political information not then known to the public, flowed back and forth as if I were not there. Finally, Humphrey took note of my presence.

"Of course, Tom," he said, "everything you're hearing here is off the record."

That's the usual, accepted rule at social affairs in Washington, or it was many years ago. But I was miffed at being taken for granted, so I sounded a warning of sorts.

"But it's all registering up here," I said as I tapped my head. "And there's a sort of statute of limitations that runs on off-the-record talk."

I won't run right out of here and write a story, I was saying. But I'm hearing it all, and I'm giving no promises for the long future. That considerably changed the course of the table talk that day. But was it a smart move? I certainly enjoyed putting those big talkers on notice. If I'd stayed silent, however, I might have learned a lot that would have been useful to me and to the *Times,* even if we couldn't rush it into print.

CHAPTER 6

Facts

In the most-watched campaign of the year 1962, Richard M. Nixon, the narrowly defeated Republican presidential candidate of 1960, mistakenly decided to run against Democrat Edmund G. "Pat" Brown, the incumbent governor of California. That year, for reasons that baffled me then and are still unclear, James Reston and his No. 2 person in the Washington bureau, Wallace Carroll, took me off the White House beat and assigned me as the *Times* national political correspondent.

Wearing my new political hat, I headed straight for California, checked into the Los Angeles Hilton and sought out my political-writer colleagues — in the bar, naturally. There, sure enough, I found the venerable Edward Folliard of *The Washington Post,* a splendid political reporter with experience dating back to FDR and Harry Truman. I explained that I was new on the beat and asked rather reverently, "Mr. Folliard, what advice can you give me?"

Eddie took a sip of his martini, thought the matter over and delivered what at first I thought was a joking response: "Young man . . . never let the facts get in your way."

Not taking seriously what proved to be sound advice, I violated it right away, though I didn't realize my error until years later. I had boarded a Nixon campaign train (the "whistle stop" was not yet entirely supplanted by the airplane) and rode it along a stretch of the West Coast. At each stop, John Chancellor (years later the NBC anchorman), other reporters and I raced to the rear of the train to hear the former vice president make a brief speech.

I reported these remarks — "the facts" — accurately enough, but I missed the better story. Nixon began every talk with the same one or two jokes, which I've mercifully forgotten. Mrs. Pat Nixon, standing dutifully behind her famous husband, would invariably laugh at each, her hands clasped tightly before her and the same pained expression on her face, mutely exclaiming: *If he tells that joke one more time, I'll scream.*

This personal example of political life, this small insight into the Nixon marriage, did not make it into my stories. I was letting the facts get in my way. But as the year wore on, I began to appreciate Eddie Folliard's wisdom.

Another notable 1962 campaign was that of Edward M. Kennedy in Massachusetts. Making his first run for his brother John's old U.S. Senate seat, Kennedy was favored to win in a close race against Eddie McCormack, whose uncle John then was Speaker of the U.S. House of Representatives. Two Massachusetts political dynasties were in mortal combat.

The first election returns to arrive in Boston, where I was reporting the story, came from Pittsfield in western Massachusetts. They showed McCormack narrowly ahead of the president's brother. Was an upset in the making? I asked John Fenton, my colleague from the *Times* New England bureau.

He took one look at the report and shook his head: "It'll be Kennedy by a landslide."

I was skeptical but Fenton reassured me: "Pittsfield's McCormack country. If Kennedy's close up there, he'll carry the state going away."

Taking his word for it, I refused this time to let the facts get in my way. Fenton proved right as usual, and in its early first edition that night, the *Times* had a page-one "beat" — "Kennedy by a Landslide." It appeared under my byline even though John Fenton really deserved the credit.

"Just the facts" is the boast of Objective Journalism, as if facts necessarily reflect truth. And "just give us the facts" is the constant plea of a public that believes anything more than the facts must be slanted, calculated to suggest or even to produce support for one side of a proposition or another.

Most journalists have had to learn, however, that the facts, even undisputed facts, can also be slanted and often are. Suppose a mayor says that the admission fee to the municipal swimming pool must be raised by $1 a head in order to keep the facility open all summer. He says it not only on the record but on television. That is a fact, therefore, something that is known and undisputed. But if left with that fact alone, the public may never learn, or may learn too late, that the additional revenue actually will be used to raise the salary of the mayor's cousin, the pool manager.

This hypothetical story exemplifies a multitude of actual political frauds and journalistic sins, in which unquestioned facts deceive a public that believes it has been fully and fairly informed by Objective Journalism.

The most egregious example of such deception in modern times, one of the darkest chapters in the history of the American press, began to take shape on Feb. 9, 1950. On that day, Senator Joseph R. McCarthy, Republican of Wisconsin, made a Lincoln's Birthday speech to the Women's Republican Club of Wheeling, W. Va. During the speech he held aloft a piece of paper charging that he had "here in my hand" the names of 205 "known Communists" in the Truman administration's Department of State.

McCarthy offered no proof and showed no one the alleged 205 names. Soon thereafter, he repeated essentially the same charge in speeches at Salt Lake City and Reno, though he cut to a perhaps more plausible 57 the number of names he supposedly held in his hand and expanded his description to "card-carrying" Communists. Back in the Senate, in a five-hour tirade, McCarthy further claimed to have penetrated the Truman administration's "iron curtain of secrecy" about Communist subversion in Washington.

In his biography *Truman,* David McCullough described Joe McCarthy as he was prior to the Wheeling speech:

> All but friendless in the Senate, recently voted the worst member . . . in a poll of Washington correspondents . . . a political brawler, morose, reckless, hard-drinking, a demagogue such as had not been seen in the Senate since the days of Huey Long, only he had none of Long's charm or brilliance . . . [t]he press called him desperate, a loudmouth and a character assassin.[1]

Joseph R. McCarthy nevertheless was a duly elected U.S. senator, an official personage, supposedly a war hero. ("Tailgunner Joe" is what some supporters had called him.) Therefore, according to the dictates of Objective Journalism, what he said, on the Senate floor or off, had to be reported as he said it. *Just the facts.* Even though McCarthy had no Communists' names and disclosed no evidence, the *fact* to be reported was that he had said what he said, made the charges he made.

---

[1] David McCullough, *Truman* (New York: Simon & Schuster, 1992), p. 765.

To go behind these few indisputable facts in search of context, or of the underlying truth about what he had said, would have been to imply that his charge was not true and at best was exaggerated and insupportable. Objective Journalism, an approach accepted at the time, would not allow such an appearance of being slanted. Most reporters knew, though, as McCullough put it, that McCarthy's so-called Communist hunt "was a wretched burlesque of the serious and necessary business of loyalty check-ups."[2] (To be objective, without the capital *O*, I should point out that McCarthy did have, and continues to have, some true believers in the "facts" he presented.)

At the time, however, letting McCarthy's charges stand unchallenged by the press, as for a long time newspapers and broadcasters mostly did, created the clear impression that what he said must be at least partially true. If not, why would he say such things? Why did no one but partisans challenge him? Of course the partisans were reported too, again without question or inquiry, leaving the public to decide whether McCarthy or his critics were telling the truth. It was an excellent, if reprehensible, case study of how facts can become slanted news when broader and more thoughtful reporting might have brought truth.

McCarthy continued for years to make, in one form or another, his mostly baseless charges, with his numbers of alleged Communists in government constantly changing. Too often, Objective Journalism simply propagated his words and just as dutifully reported — also without significant comment or context — the protests and counter-charges of the politicians, academics and others with nerve and knowledge enough to challenge Tailgunner Joe. The words of most of these people, however, seemed defensive and carried nothing like the clout of a U.S. senator who had become a sort of hero, the bold scourge of subversion.

Inevitably, McCarthy's sensational allegations, repeated and reported, too ineffectively refuted — and hardly refuted at all by the press — came to be believed by all too many Americans. Even some who did not literally accept the verbose senator's rantings came to think that he was on to something, that there must be at least some truth in what the press regularly reported him to be saying. McCarthy, braving the wrath of the powerful, became politically intimidating

---

[2] When Bill Lawrence of *The New York Times* was assigned to cover McCarthy, he quipped that he had been given "the sewer beat." William H. Lawrence, *Six Presidents, Too Many Wars* (New York: Saturday Review Press, 1972), p. 199.

even to a national icon like President Eisenhower. (In the senator's home state, Wisconsin, Eisenhower removed from a speech remarks defending General George Marshall, his revered mentor, against a baseless McCarthy attack.)

Herblock, the great cartoonist of *The Washington Post,* first used the term *McCarthyism* to connote reckless and unsubstantiated charges, "smears" without substance that nevertheless damage or destroy an opponent. That word is now common in the American language. The original McCarthyism, however, could not have flourished so profusely even in the Cold War, and the word itself probably would not have entered our language, had it not been for Objective Journalism.[3]

Am I suggesting that reporters and the press should not be objective? Of course not, especially if being objective means being fair and evenhanded. But the idea known as Objective Journalism, as I'm using the term, has little relation to the dictionary meaning of the word *objective.* It's a restrictive concept to which publishers and broadcasters once paid fervent allegiance in order to win or retain the favor of readers and viewers who apparently demanded it.

Objective Journalism insisted on "nothing but the facts" and the obvious facts at that — the text of a speech, for instance, or the record of a vote in the Senate or the House. Interpretation of any kind was seen as nonobjective at best, unfair at worst. A politician could legitimately be described as "a former governor"; he or she could *not* be described as a "former governor with liberal views." The latter description would require a conclusion, no matter how plausible, and could be construed as slanting the news for or against the governor.

Objective Journalism, therefore, was virtually indisputable; it was not open to the charge of bias — in fact, it was designed to be immune to any such charge. Objective Journalism, however, failed to give the reader or viewer any perspective, even necessary perspective, on the facts reported. George W. Bush did not win the popular vote in 2000 — that's a fact. But he won the presidential election — that's a fact, too, but one that needs explanation and perspective.

What readers and viewers didn't know or realize, though, is that Objective Journalism is not always fair and not always evenhanded.

---

[3] If the charge is overstated—some in journalism fought McCarthy hard and well—it's to make the point that the press's *general* devotion to Objective Journalism was vital to the survival of McCarthyism.

Suppose, for example, that in 1939 journalism had placed equal trust and confidence in the words and performances of Hitler and Churchill (the legal leaders of Germany and Great Britain), challenged the claims of neither, and given each exactly equal prominence on the air and in print. That might have been considered objective. But fair? Evenhanded? Hardly. Given history, experience and the knowledge of those who had closely observed both men, even by 1939 to equate Hitler and Churchill as leaders actually was to elevate Hitler, a thug and a liar, to equal stature with Churchill in integrity and intention.

Decades later, in 1963, when President Ngo Dinh Diem of South Vietnam was overthrown and assassinated in Saigon, *The New York Times* ran two measured stories of about the same length and under similar headlines, next to each other on page one. The first story, date-lined Washington, quoted officials in the capital to the effect that the Kennedy administration had not planned or authorized the coup and certainly not Diem's murder. The other story, datelined Saigon, quoted sources there as saying that Diem's murder had been the inescapable result of a coup planned and authorized in Washington. The reader could decide which article to believe.

In that case, editors probably couldn't be sure which story was the most reliable. Printing both with equal prominence in order to give two sides of a story may therefore have been a rational — if not, as time disclosed, a correct — solution. In many cases, however, strict adherence to the concept of Objective Journalism results in unfairness for all involved. This is because Objective Journalism is a rather cring-ing concept designed *to avoid criticism from either side.*

Those in Washington in 1963 who denied complicity in Diem's death could hardly complain too loudly about the conflicting story from Saigon, or vice versa, since the view of each had been given full and equal treatment. If either version had been printed to the disadvan-tage of the other, the offended side would have cried foul, or so editors feared. Never mind how the reader was supposed to figure out what actually had happened. Whose story was the reader to believe? If both sides were covered, then so was the *Times'* posterior.

Here's another hypothetical:
Suppose the president of the United States proposes a bill to revoke the licenses of real-estate agents who can be proved guilty of the "racial steering" of blacks away from available housing in white

neighborhoods. You're a Washington reporter assigned to write the story for the evening news.

Conscientiously, you telephone Senator Stonewall of Mississippi and ask him for his opinion. With an eye on his constituency, he's happy, for once, to speak on the record:

> That bill's terrible, an outrage. Real-estate licenses are not a federal responsibility. This misguided proposal would invade states' rights, attack local custom, unconstitutionally interfere in private business, and is just a political bid for black votes in the cities.

You duly note all this. Maybe you've even taped Stonewall's statement, having told him, as required by law, that you were doing so. Then you call Senator Sobhart of Massachusetts. His opinion is equally clear, and he too agrees to speak on the record because his views won't hurt him in New England:

> About time we did something about housing segregation. A justified intervention under the interstate commerce clause. These states-righters want to keep African-Americans segregated so they can rake in a lot of right-wing votes.

You get both quotations high up in your story, just after a lead that briefly lays out what's in the president's bill. Then, as space permits, you more carefully detail the proposal, including more objections to it and praise for it, and write a final wrap-up sentence:

> Thus sectional strife threatens to engulf a Congress already divided and feuding on partisan issues even before the president handed it this new challenge.

If you've been trained in the ways of Objective Journalism, you've done your job. You've stated the issue, quoted the opinions on both sides fully and without suggestive editorial comment, provided roughly equal play for Stonewall and Sobhart, outlined the details so that readers or viewers can decide for themselves, and suggested that a fight is brewing.

There are, of course, other ways to handle this particular story. For instance, after your lead, you could offer statistics about racial steering. Is it prevalent? Is it really a factor in continued housing segregation?

You could also seek out some acknowledged nonpolitical authorities on the Constitution to discuss whether the president's proposal really does invade states' rights.

If so, you could do some research on what any of the states might have done to stop racial steering. And what has the real-estate profession done? Judging from precedent, what's the Supreme Court likely to say?

The two senators' differing responses surely would gain perspective from such additional information. Your audience might even be helped in reaching its own judgments if you provided more than the details of the bill and of the conflicting reactions.

Unfortunately, if you followed any of these latter approaches, or a combination of some of them, your story's expanded context might tend to support either the Stonewall or the Sobhart view. And you might have pushed or pulled the reader or viewer in whatever direction your research and reporting might suggest.

You'd perhaps appear, moreover, to be violating one of the shibboleths of journalism, to which the public is deeply devoted and to which newspapers and broadcasters often pay fervent lip service. You would not have "let the facts speak for themselves," as Objective Journalism requires.

Following the tenets of Objective Journalism often means accepting rather obvious facts and reporting them without further comment or context, even if that's misleading. My life in the trade has taught me that journalists should think less about this kind of objectivity and more about being evenhanded.

Being evenhanded means offering truly equal treatment of conflicting arguments or personalities, including context, precedent and possible consequences. Evenhandedness often requires a wider quest for differing views, a willingness to put events into a context that may be unfamiliar to readers or viewers and an effort to reach whatever truth may lie behind surface facts. Sometimes it will risk the charge of "editorializing" by applying the reporter's own knowledge and experience to his or her account.

Let's look at a more familiar example:

If a reporter were writing evenhandedly about the Clinton-Bush presidential campaign in 1992, he or she certainly should have known from even cursory research or limited experience that only one Democrat — Jimmy Carter in 1976 — had been elected president in the 28 years since the Johnson landslide of 1964. Should that reporter not have put that fact into the story? Even if it did suggest a national Republican trend or that in 1992 the Democrats had little chance?

Suppose the reporter had concluded from research and experience that there was a reason for the Democrats' long record of electoral futility and an obvious one at that: The Democrats consistently had put up weak candidates (Hubert Humphrey, George McGovern, an unsuccessful President Jimmy Carter in 1980, Walter Mondale, Michael Dukakis). Should the reporter not have put that in the story?

If the reporter did attempt to establish such a context, should he or she have put the facts in the mouth of a political science professor or a so-called political expert or have quoted the *World Almanac*? In other words, should the reporter have stayed "out of the story," as editors steeped in Objective Journalism used to insist?[4]

This approach tells reporters it's better to invent a euphemism or find (or invent?) a source than to bring their own knowledge into open play. Thus, even though a reporter has personal knowledge of a politician's tendency to flip-flop rather than stand on principle, the reporter might nevertheless feel compelled to write the following:

> Colleagues say Rep. Floppola has a reputation for counting proponents and adversaries before committing himself to any controversial proposition.

Obviously, this kind of dodge distorts the point and relies on unidentified sources — those unnamed colleagues. And the reader has no way of knowing if Floppola actually has such a reputation among colleagues, whether or not they were queried, or if they actually exist.

Many a reporter has had to resort to such a formulation, which is hardly a service to the reader or viewer, in order to circumvent the boundaries of Objective Journalism. Actually, if a reporter had expressed in a story about the 1992 election his or her personal experience of the previous quarter-century of presidential politics, that would not have been editorializing at all. On the contrary, the reporter would have been citing an experience that a reader should not be expected to have and knowledge that a political reporter for a leading newspaper *should* be expected to have.

---

[4] Objective Journalism is not today nearly the norm it once was in news reporting. Particularly in magazine journalism, splendid reporters like Tom Wolfe, Nicholas Lemann and others routinely and effectively put themselves and their experiences in getting the story at the center of their articles.

The reporter would be editorializing only if he or she expressed *opinion* in a supposedly evenhanded story. Of course, a reporter has no business openly urging the election of a candidate or the passage of a bill, no matter how knowledgeably he or she may be able to discuss either. A reporter has a profound responsibility, however, to report more than just surface facts, such as that a candidate is running or that he's been the governor of a major state. And to provide a context for such facts, where may a reporter better turn than to his or her own hard-won experience and knowledge?

Proponents of Objective Journalism, both in and out of the craft, assert confidently that it's too easy for reporters to slip opinion into a story in the guise of experience. If reporters can even partially escape the strictures of Objective Journalism, proponents argue, they will slide all the way into editorializing.

I suppose some would, and some have. But I've often seen reporters of strong and openly stated personal preferences (at the bar or on the press bus) suppress such opinions in the press room in order to write evenhanded accounts of speeches, campaigns, controversies and candidates. Even some whose articles served to support Joe McCarthy could not, in personal conversations, entirely hide their distaste for his falsehoods.

Objective Journalism is the pretense, by public and press alike, that news reports can and should be untainted by any point of view except that of a publicly committed person. News reports are to be unsullied by any but indisputable facts, unshaded by historical or economic or social context, and unshaped by reporters' predilections and experiences.

If that were possible, Objective Journalism would be virtually untouched by human hands or thought. Instead, it would rattle unchallenged from some soulless, mindless machine, like prices from the market ticker. But such an "ideal" is not possible; it is only advocated.

Reporters are not automatons or computer chips or mere news "tickers." They are human beings, different in relatively superficial ways from bankers, doctors, construction workers or politicians. They have families as well as careers and were raised in conditions of poverty or affluence or something between. Most reporters nowadays have a college education but are in lower income brackets than their educational peers — higher brackets, however, than most blue- and many white-collar Americans. Like others in this country, journalists derive their social, political and moral views from their parents and from childhood and life experiences. More and more, in recent years, reporters and editors are women, in what is happily becoming a gender-free craft. In that, too, journalists are more like than different from other Americans.

All of this is not to say that journalists are just like other people. No one would profess more loudly than I that they can't be pinned down like butterflies on cardboard. Journalists really are something of a breed apart: curious, skeptical, suspicious, independent, irreverent and more in love with their work than most. But so much diversity of political and social outlook and economic status exists among them that it's silly to consider them all — as many Americans apparently do — leftists, elitists, Democrats, internationalists or, even worse, dishonest and slaves to the almighty dollar. Some journalists may be any or even all of those things, but so might many other Americans.

To proclaim, therefore, as some brass hats of the press are fond of doing, that any member of this diverse group can sit down to a keyboard and bang out a flawlessly objective story is like decreeing that snow will fall on the Sahara. All reporters bring to that keyboard their life experiences and professional backgrounds. They may bring a political affiliation, an organization's operating rules, a familiarity or lack of familiarity with the people and events they are writing about, a rebellious or satisfied attitude toward politics and society, an optimistic or pessimistic nature, and not least their parents' admonitions, applied or ignored. In short, each reporter is a personality, not a blank slot into which a punched tape can be fed.

Therefore, I insist, no reporter can prevent what he or she *is* from creeping into a story. Who could? Can the business leader or schoolteacher cast aside what he or she is? Whatever life has made of individuals, for better or for worse, is reflected in their attitudes and expression, and journalists are no exception. It is inevitable, then, that life experience will be reflected in a journalist's work, not in bald statements of opinion or bursts of editorial urgings (both properly prohibited in news reporting) but rather in word choice, emphasis, detail and inflection.

A suspicious public that sniffs for slanted news, as a bloodhound seeks the scent of a fleeing convict in a footprint, may perceive deliberate slanting in the inescapable fact that no reporter can entirely obliterate what he or she *is* — conservative, optimist, affluent, ill-educated — from the work being written. Usually, however, slanting is in the olfactory organ of the sniffer. Slanting does, of course, occur, but usually it is a result of deliberate intent. Reporters are trained in, and take pride in, the discipline of holding themselves above palpable, immediate influences, such as whether they favor a particular candidate or party or personally dislike the president. They consider detachment from such obvious influences as a mark of their craft, their integrity.

As a rule, White House reporters don't stand up, as audiences generally do, when the band plays "Hail to the Chief." This is not because they don't respect the president or they lack patriotism but because they're reluctant to show deference to anyone or to any office. Besides, presidents come and go.

John Herbers of *The New York Times* once was called on the carpet by President Johnson's press secretary, George Christian, and berated for supposed errors in a story Herbers regarded as fair and accurate. Herbers, who had covered Mississippi during the worst of the civil rights upheaval, was not intimidated. He was annoyed, however, at being "summoned to stand accused," even at a president's behest.

Unfortunately, polls and surveys disclose that Americans who rail against the supposedly "liberal press" often deeply suspect that reporters deliberately, even usually, slant the news, often under orders from editors or publishers or advertisers or all of them. Such poll results cause nervous official voices of the press, in their anxiety to avoid criticism, to extol Objective Journalism, which is what the public seems to want to hear but seldom believes.

These official press spokespersons insist that Americans really do get the news "straight." That proposition leads, however, to a question neither press moguls nor the reading and viewing public likes to dwell on: What *is* straight news?

Is it the surface facts of an event? The text of a speech? Can news be straight if it's not put into a sensible context? If a politician promises a tax cut, is it straight news to report the promise without pointing out that a deficit might result, or that a majority in the relevant legislative body is opposed to cutting taxes, or that some will get a bigger tax cut than others?

Journalists generally know through hard experience that providing a fair, full and evenhanded account of almost any event is not a simple matter of reciting indisputable facts. Even a football game may have been played quite differently from what the score and the statistics suggest and from what fans could see from the seats.

Catching the nuance, the complexity, painting in the background —
like Pat Nixon's desperate smile — suggesting the context, even specu-
lating plausibly on the consequences, doing all of this fairly and evenhandedly: These are the reporter's real challenge, the prime obligations
of the press. But such goals cannot be met by the simplicities and rigid-
ity of Objective Journalism as it's popularly conceived.

CHAPTER 7

Eyewitnesses

Not every reporter sees and/or hears everything about which he or she must write a story. That luxury is the province of sports reporters in the press box, or perhaps the political writer at the governor's inaugural, or the fashion expert watching long-stemmed beauties parading on the runway at the Paris showings. Even these reporters don't always know the whole story behind the event they're watching. The sports reporter, for instance, may not know that the quarterback is playing so furiously because he's been told privately that his starter's job is in danger of being handed to a talented backup.

Reporters are more often in the position of the journalism student in Russell Baker's imagination. A brilliant writer and an experienced Washington reporter, first for *The Baltimore Sun* and then for *The New York Times,* Baker once described the comprehensive journalism course that he proposed every aspiring reporter should be required to take.

The student would stand with a group of his or her peers outside a closed door for, say, three hours. Then the door would open. Someone looking rather like Senator Trent Lott of Mississippi or Alan Greenspan of the Federal Reserve would put his head momentarily around the jamb to announce curtly: "No comment."

Whereupon the head would disappear, the door would close and the student reporter — lacking time even to interview people as they emerged — would have to dash back to the newsroom and write 600 words against a deadline.

Baker was joking, of course. But the truth is that an experienced reporter actually could pass his test (Russ Baker himself better than most) and probably often has.

After all, the reporter (even if a student) knew *why* he or she was standing in front of that closed door. Something considered "news" was going on in there. The gathered reporters had at least some idea about *who* was inside and knew in a general way *what* was supposed to be happening. They might also have known, then, what decision was be expected. Given that background to start with, even "no comment" would tell an alert reporter quite a lot. At the very least, it would indicate that those meeting behind the closed door didn't want to tell the public what they had done or failed to do. If the group had voted to cut taxes or to do something equally popular, they would want to grab the credit.

If the reporter were experienced and well-enough informed to begin with, his or her 600-word story might make page one — and it might even tell the reader something useful. After all, in a given set of circumstances, nothing happening can be as informative as something happening — Barry Bonds didn't hit another home run or the tax bill was not approved.

Besides, a reporter can always use the telephone to try to get more information. Much of the time there's a leaker just waiting for the chance to influence or even "make" the news, especially if the leaker has the field to him- or herself. After the reporter's vigil and quick dismissal, experience would instruct him or her to get quickly on the phone and quiz someone who might say more than "no comment." Experience might also suggest a possible leaker who would wish to glorify his or her own participation in whatever happened or didn't, or to blow the whistle (in secret, of course) on colleagues' action or lack of it.

In short, above and beyond that bureaucratic "no comment" (familiar words to journalists!), an informed and determined reporter has the most useful tools of the trade — background, experience and instinct — with which to rise above that head in the doorway.

On Nov. 22, 1963, as the *Times* White House correspondent, I was far back, in the second of three press buses, in the lengthy motorcade making its way through Dallas in the wake of President Kennedy's limousine. As I recall, at least a dozen vehicles were between the second bus and that ill-fated limo. Consequently, I saw nothing of what happened far ahead and didn't know that Kennedy had been shot. I was unaware even that *anything* had happened until Jim Mathis, a colleague who had left his seat beside me to stand in front of the bus, hurried back to where I was sitting.

"The president's car just sped off," Mathis exclaimed. "Really gunned away!"

Moments before, our bus had rounded a corner into what became well known as Dealey Plaza, and it had started toward what the world was to learn was the Texas School Book Depository. The crowd gathered in the plaza to watch the motorcade passage of President and Mrs. Kennedy had suddenly dispersed. People were running about, aimless and obviously alarmed, spilling over the street and through the park-like plaza.

Something plainly had happened, but for all I or other reporters in the second press bus knew, it might have been no more than someone braving the Secret Service escort to throw an egg at the president (Dallas being then considered the right-wing capital of the world). Or, if a more serious threat had arisen, the leading vehicles in the motorcade and the White House limousine might be racing ahead to escape any possible danger.

Believe it or not, those of us in that second press bus — and I think most reporters in the first bus — did not learn that Kennedy had been shot until a few minutes later. Except for the presidential limousine, the rest of the motorcade went directly to the Dallas Trade Mart, where Kennedy had been scheduled to speak at a mammoth luncheon. In the great hall of the Trade Mart, we reporters literally could *see* some sort of rumor sweeping over the assembled crowd. Then, in a makeshift upstairs press room, Marianne Means of the Hearst newspapers routinely called her office in New York.

"My God!" an excited voice replied. "Don't you know the president's been shot?"

Until then, none of us did. (This is an example of the advantages of broadcasting over print; radio bulletins actually had reached the East Coast before some of us in Texas had learned the terrible news.)

I see no need to repeat here the thousands of words I've written about that day in Dallas, except to make the point that I've already described *all* that I actually *saw* of Kennedy's assassination. The only other eyewitness material I got that day was a brief glimpse of Jacqueline Kennedy with blood on her stocking and her hand on her husband's coffin as it was wheeled out of Parkland Hospital on the way to *Air Force One* on the runway at the old Dallas Love Field.

One relatively unimportant incident does stand out in my mind. As reporters eventually reached the hospital, still unaware that Kennedy was dead, we encountered Senator Ralph Yarborough, Democrat of Texas, in the parking lot. With his political adversary, Vice President Lyndon B. Johnson, Yarborough had been riding in the car just behind the president's. Kennedy's purpose in coming to Texas had been partially to make peace between those warring Democrats, in anticipation of a Kennedy-Johnson reelection campaign in 1964.

"Gentlemen," Senator Yarborough, an old-school orator, told us in words engraved on my memory, "it is a deed of horror."

We reporters then received a hurried briefing from Parkland doctors, although some of their information, which we had no time to check, turned out to be inaccurate. We also received a "pool" report from Sid Davis, a Westinghouse radio reporter who had got himself aboard *Air Force One* during the swearing in of Lyndon Johnson. Davis got off the plane before it took off for Washington, then climbed on the hood of a parked automobile to brief the rest of us.

With not much more solid information than that, I wrote a story that covered two page-one columns and an entire inside page of the *Times*. It was not a unique feat, but I'm proud of the work I did under that day's pressures. In such fluid and extraordinary circumstances, a reporter has to rely not merely on information (certainly not on *eyewitness* information) but also on background, experience and instinct. I had to rely mostly on instinct and experience, for instance, to distinguish plausible information out of the welter of rumor and report that swamped the Dallas airwaves. One breathless radio reporter actually shouted to his audience that "President Kennedy was killed today in Big D!"

To give you a more useful example, I heard on radio that the Dallas police had arrested a suspect. Rather than chasing this down — true or false?; and if true, whom and why? — I kept on writing the basic assassination story. Later, the *Times* national desk in New York inserted, from wire-service reports, the details of Lee Harvey Oswald's arrest in a movie theater and why it was suspected that he had committed the murder though he repeatedly denied it.

Because of that radio report, I was able, moreover, to cite the arrest to Gladwin Hill, the *Times* Los Angeles correspondent, who was the first reporter to fly into Dallas to help me. When Hill arrived at Love Field, I was at work in the terminal building (in those precomputer days) on my Olivetti portable typewriter. On my advice, Hill went to the police station, remained there all weekend and was an eyewitness (that rarity!) on Sunday to Oswald's murder by Jack Ruby.

Background, experience and instinct are more often the basis of reporting than is visual observation. That was certainly the case for me that day in Dallas. Except for some sportswriters, reporters usually have to piece together a story after the event, using various accounts that are not always dispassionate and too frequently self-serving. They may also use the official record, if any, which sometimes comes from television film. Perhaps most important is what reporters know of human nature and motives and of the political or military environment of the event.

None of these, unfortunately, not even an explicit image or an official record, necessarily tells a reporter the whole truth. Nothing does. Reporters still must work with what they have, learn what they can and tell what they believe.

On a Sunday night in August 1964, I sat in front of a TV in the Washington bureau of the *Times* to cover a speech by President Johnson. In his customarily menacing manner, he told the nation that attacks had been carried out by North Vietnamese vessels against U.S. naval forces in the Gulf of Tonkin.

These attacks led the Johnson administration to retaliate with bombing runs on North Vietnam and heightened the pressure that was to cause Congress to approve the now-infamous Tonkin Gulf resolution. It gave Johnson (as he but not all members of Congress interpreted it) virtual carte blanche to fight what became the war in Vietnam. History now indicates that the president's report that Sunday night of a second attack in the Tonkin Gulf probably was not true — or at least may not have been true.

Even Robert S. McNamara, who was secretary of defense in 1964, wrote later that "evidence of the first attack [on Aug. 2] is indisputable. The second attack [on Aug. 4] appears probable but not certain."[1]

Had LBJ lied, then, to the nation? Or been lied to by the Pentagon? Might the Defense Department itself have been lied to by its agents in Vietnam? Or had some disastrous misunderstanding occurred somewhere along the line?

I'm still not certain what happened. But unlike McNamara, I didn't think the attack was "probable." And more to the point for me that August night: *What was I to do?* I only suspected (based on my background, experience and instinct), but I did not know — and certainly could not prove — that the second attack had not taken place.

Furthermore, since it was nearing midnight on Sunday, most sources of information were not available. Those officials who might

---

[1] Robert S. McNamara, with Brian VanDeMark, *In Retrospect* (New York: Random House/Times Books, 1995), p. 128. In this work, McNamara presented detailed evidence that administration officials were uncertain even at the time that the second "attack" was, in fact, an attack.

have taken a phone call at that hour either would have been primed to corroborate the president or would know nothing pro or con about the supposed attack. Keep in mind that this episode occurred 34 years before Bill Clinton wagged his forefinger at the camera and denied having sexual relations with "that woman." In those days, any president — then even LBJ, who was to be widely mistrusted later — was regarded as an unimpeachable authority when he spoke to the nation in his official capacity.[2]

So, after a few fruitless phone calls, I yielded to circumstance and frustration. I reported the speech as Lyndon Johnson had given it, and I still don't see what sound alternative I had. But in thousands of libraries and archives, easily available to the future, lies the microfiche record of that misleading story with my byline on it.

A scholar someday might ask: "How could an experienced reporter like Wicker propagate a disputed, maybe phony story like that?"

He or she probably won't understand or credit the circumstances under which I was working. Background, experience and instinct, which had led me — uncertainly, I admit — through Dallas on Nov. 22, 1963, raised warnings but could not sustain them on the night of President Johnson's speech. I had to fall back on the official record, the televised speech that I and the nation had seen and heard. And I did so even though I had already learned to my sorrow that the record is not always the same as the truth.

Even documents and photographs can tell an untrue story, can be made to lie. This dispiriting truth was brought home to me nearly a half-century ago, before the success of the civil rights movement, when I was the sports editor of the *Winston-Salem (N.C.) Journal.* It was then locally owned and a frequent prize winner for excellence of various kinds, but its circulation area, significantly, was limited to northwestern North Carolina and southern Virginia.

Holding down the *Journal* sports desk in 1954 was an instructive step in my budding journalistic career. For one thing, it taught me that

---

[2] Presidential lying did not begin with Clinton. President Eisenhower was caught in a lie when he first said an American U-2 that had been shot down over the Soviet Union in 1960 was flying a "weather mission." The public seemed to forgive him. Later, from my press conference seat in the front row as *The New York Times* White House correspondent, I asked President Kennedy directly, "Are American troops now in combat in Vietnam?" He stared at me a moment and then said flatly, "No." He knew it was a lie and I believed it was, but the public probably thought it was true.

what may be fascinating to a fan — of baseball or football or even politics — can be a bore to those too often exposed to it. In that year, moreover, the extension of the coaxial cable (harbinger of technological transformations to come!) permitted the World Series, for the first time, to be televised in the South. This, of course, made the Series even more intensely interesting to our sports-mad circulation area than when it had been broadcast only on radio.

In 1954, the New York Giants, in a resounding Series upset, swept the Cleveland Indians in four straight games. Willie Mays, the youthful Giants centerfielder, was a new star. After the final game, one of the wire services provided a photo of Mays and the Giants manager, Leo Durocher, celebrating in the locker room. I routinely scheduled the photo for prominent play on the first sports page. Worth Bacon, the managing editor, an unlucky poker player but a knowledgeable journalist, looked over my layout and asked to see the photo. He studied it for a while and shook his head gravely at the sight of Mays' black arm around Durocher's white shoulder.

I had forgotten, but Worth Bacon hadn't, that in late 1954 North Carolina and the rest of the South were still segregated, TV or no TV, and no matter what the Supreme Court recently had said in *Brown vs. Board of Education*. When that Series picture ran on the sports page that night, however, white Southern baseball fans had no cause to complain about the *Journal* encouraging racial fraternization because Willie Mays' arm around Durocher's shoulder had been painted out.

Worth Bacon was an eminently decent man reacting to his environment. His decision may have been a little extreme, even for the time and place, but doctored photographs were not then and still aren't rarities in the news. And as technology has advanced light years beyond the coaxial cable, the degree of such fakery on television, the Internet and in print has risen and will continue to rise, exponentially. When a TV commercial can re-create on film an apparently alive and threatening John Wayne, after the real "Duke" has been dead and buried for years, and when CBS can make its logo appear to be painted on the wall of the General Motors building, what might be expected next?

No reporter knows more certainly that the record is not always the truth than the so-called investigative reporter. These reporters came into public notoriety mostly after Bob Woodward and Carl Bernstein rose to fame with their Watergate reporting and were portrayed on screen by Robert Redford and Dustin Hoffman.

Actually, most reporters, at one time or another, are investigative reporters. Aside from the rare eyewitness story, most reporting is investigation. And sometimes when a reporter literally has seen something happen, he or she still has to make inquiries — sometimes requiring days or months — to learn the sequence or meaning of events precisely, certainly to find out *why,* or perhaps *who,* caused the happening, what might be its consequences, and so on.

Accurately reporting the yeas and nays in a Senate vote, for example, or the raw figures in an unemployment survey, is sometimes the least of the story beneath these facts. It's not too much to say that every reporter is an investigative reporter or may have to become one on any given assignment.

Still, so impressive were the feats of Woodward and Bernstein, and so glittering was their fame in the wake of Richard Nixon's resignation and William Goldman's movie script[3] about Watergate, that a virtual fad for investigative reporting was born in the seventies — as if no such thing had been heard of before. Newspapers and broadcasters that for years had had reporters or teams at work on various investigations began to publicize this kind of work as a new and admirable departure for journalism. Even some newspapers and broadcasters who had never inquired into anything more than some politician's voting record suddenly discovered virtue and anointed a reporter or a team of them as journalistic investigators.

To some extent, the sudden notoriety of investigative reporting caused those engaged in it to be more nearly set apart than they had been in the past, like swat teams in police work or designated hitters in the American League. In most cases, however, investigative reporting was not really new; it just had new status and in some cases a boastful, often absurd new team title, like the Spy Squad or the Snoop Troop. Often, special logos were devised to differentiate investigative stories from what once had been routine news reporting.

Much of this was pretentious. On the whole, though, the "Woodstein" craze — aside from giving journalism briefly enhanced status and enlarging enrollments at journalism schools — made journalists more aware of the need to dig behind the scenes. It also gave reporters who wrote publicized investigative stories greater credibility with the public.

Some reporters then or earlier developed an investigative specialty and were seldom asked to work on more routine stories. Others, like

---

[3] *All the President's Men,* 1976.

Wallace Turner, a Pulitzer Prize winner and San Francisco bureau chief for *The New York Times,* remained versatile general reporters who could also bird-dog an investigative story. Turner dug up such a story when he exposed Richard Nixon's use of government funds to improve his West Coast villa.

In the footsteps of Woodward and Bernstein, some reporters probing iniquity or mispractice became famous as investigative specialists. Seymour Hersh, for example, brought to light the My Lai massacre in Vietnam and later uncovered some illicit activities of the Central Intelligence Agency in its glory days.

Investigative reporting has its critics, as does almost every form of journalism. One criticism is that the so-called investigative reporter sometimes becomes a "true believer," so engaged with a story, so convinced that if he or she looks hard enough and long enough the necessary evidence of wrongdoing surely will be found, that it *must* be available to determined quest. Such a true believer may even go to press or on the air with a story inadequately proven or at least doubtful in some of its elements. It's not that an investigative reporter deliberately falsifies the facts. Most are not only honest but fiercely dedicated to the exposure of evildoing. Rather, it's that such a reporter has become so convinced of a certain truth that insufficient evidence, conclusive only in his or her mind, may come to seem final and sufficient.

A more frequently heard reservation is whether a reporter is ethically entitled to pretend to be something or someone he or she is not, in order to prove a story that can't be adequately documented through ordinary means. Should a practice like impersonating an officer or forging a check not be permitted? Or are such practices a legitimate means of exposing corruption and serving the public?

On Nov. 5, 1992, a magazine news program on ABC-TV, *Prime Time Live,* with the popular Diane Sawyer as anchor, presented a segment charging that a supermarket chain, Food Lion, sold tainted chicken, cheese, beef and fish. ABC News was able to do the story because two of its journalists had falsely filled out employment forms and obtained jobs as food handlers with Food Lion. The journalists then used cameras concealed on their persons to record evidence that supermarket employees, in the words of a federal judge, "were repackaging and redating fish that had passed the expiration date, grinding expired beef with fresh beef and applying barbecue sauce to chicken to mask the smell and sell it as fresh."

After the story aired, Food Lion's stock price dropped by 20 percent, and its sales fell by more than 9 percent in one month. Predictably, the food chain (which is based in North Carolina) sued ABC for $2 billion in damages, charging that the two journalists had used deception to get their jobs and then trespassed on Food Lion property to prove their story. Unpredictably, Food Lion did not sue for libel or contest the truth of the ABC News charges.

On Jan. 23, 1997, more than four years after the broadcast, a North Carolina jury awarded Food Lion $5.5 million in punitive damages, after having earlier allowed the chain only $1,402 in actual damages. In August 1997, the trial judge cut the punitive-damages award to $315,000, thus limiting Food Lion's recovery to far less than the $2 billion originally sought. The same judge had admonished the trial jury to focus on the charges of fraud, trespass and disloyalty and to disregard any question of journalistic rights and responsibilities. Nevertheless, the original jury foreman had solemnly declared that the verdict was meant to send a message to the media that it should be responsible.

ABC appealed the verdict. In November 1999, a federal appeals court in Richmond, Va., threw out all but $2 of the earlier judgment — $1 for the trespass and $1 for violating a North Carolina statute requiring employees to be loyal to the company they work for. ABC was required to pay nothing, however, for libel or false reporting.

Did ABC News and journalism therefore win the case? Was underground reporting justified? Well, sort of, but not exactly.

For one thing, opinion polls showed rather conclusively that the public agreed with the original jury that the journalists' tactics had been unacceptably deceptive. I had a personal taste of this attitude while I was teaching a class of nonjournalism students at Davidson College in the autumn of 1997, before the final Richmond verdict. Most of the students in that class expressed outrage not at Food Lion's undenied marketing practices but at the admitted deceptions of ABC News.

For another thing, even journalists were divided over the propriety of the ABC journalists' actions. Some believed the network had pushed the story primarily to build ratings. This is a common charge against television and newspapers but not one usually heard from within. Other journalists thought that reporters masquerading as food handlers while using hidden cameras was carrying underground journalism too far. Again, this was an attitude not often found among journalists themselves. Television's frequent use of hidden cameras and ambush interviews — in which someone, presumably unprepared, suddenly finds him- or herself being interrogated on camera — may have made such procedures unpopular in some journalists' minds.

For still a third thing, the Fourth Circuit Court of Appeals in Richmond did not even mention, in its final judgment, the First Amendment or the rights of the press or its responsibilities to the public. The Food Lion suit had focused on the chain's fraud claim against the network, and it was for that charge, not for libel or false statements, that the $5.5 million in punitive damages originally was awarded.

Nor did ABC's lawyers plead the First Amendment. They argued instead that Food Lion had not proved its fraud claim and therefore that punitive damages could not be awarded. Moreover, based on a history of notoriously impermanent and unreliable job applicants, the Fourth Circuit ruled that Food Lion could not reasonably have expected the two journalists who posed as food handlers to work longer than the two weeks they were actually on the chain's payroll. So there was no fraud, and consequently there could be no punitive damages for the mere allegation of fraud.

In only one respect could the Richmond ruling be construed as a First Amendment victory. The appeals court did uphold the trial court's refusal to allow Food Lion to collect for defamation damages unless it could prove that ABC News had knowingly broadcast false statements of fact or had recklessly declined to determine whether its statements were true or false. This ruling only conformed, however, to First Amendment law previously established by the Supreme Court.

Thus, the ABC victory was primarily for ABC News and not for journalism in general. The Fourth Circuit did not establish or recognize any special protection for news gathering, particularly not for deceptive reporting practices, even in cases of vital public interest. Nor did it rule that the truthfulness of a story is a valid defense against fraud, trespass or similar charges.[4]

Actually, underground or undercover journalism was nothing new when *Prime Time Live* took on Food Lion. In 1888, Nellie Bly had exposed the ill-treatment of the insane on Blackwell's Island, New York, by posing as one of them. In 1928, journalist Tom Howard had

---

[4] For this analysis of the various rulings in the Food Lion case, I am indebted to material provided by the First Amendment Center of the Freedom Forum, funded by the Gannett Foundation.

strapped a camera to his ankle to photograph surreptitiously the execution of Ruth Snyder, the first woman to die in the electric chair. In another famous case, the *Chicago Sun-Times* had bought part ownership of the Mirage Bar, planted reporters as bartenders and waiters, and used their eavesdrop evidence to expose bribery and corruption in local government.

ABC News itself had used undercover tactics to expose abusive conditions in Texas, Ohio and Louisiana institutions as well as racial steering by real-estate agents. Hidden cameras have also been used by various news agencies to document certain security problems at airports and hospitals. John Seigenthaler, formerly a resourceful investigative reporter himself and later the editor and publisher of Nashville's *The Tennessean*, once assigned a reporter to infiltrate the Ku Klux Klan. Under cover of secrecy, the reporter was able to prove that the Klan was racist and armed and to portray David Duke — who later became a political candidate in Louisiana — as a committed Klansman. For another undercover story, one of Seigenthaler's reporters, Frank Sutherland, posed as potentially suicidal, spent 30 days in Tennessee's Central State Hospital and reported not only neglect and abuse of patients but that half the staff doctors were not licensed to practice in the state.

Under Seigenthaler, *The Tennessean* had a three-point policy governing such "deceptions." The evil being investigated had to be of compelling public interest; no other way could be found to report the story in its entirety; and the undercover tactics had to be disclosed when the story was published.[5]

There is a long history of effective underground journalism (only a few examples of which have been cited here), and journalism has been able to perform many public services as a result. I find it hard to disagree with John Seigenthaler's dictum that "sometimes journalists should be allowed to tell a small lie in order to expose a large evil," particularly under the three points of control he exercised in Nashville. I fully recognize, however, that much, perhaps most, of the reading and viewing public does not share this view. Indeed, many people find it ironic or worse that in claiming only to seek the truth journalism sometimes engages in untruth.

But even when journalistic deceptions are effective and in the public interest, like that practiced by ABC News in the Food Lion case,

---

[5] The Gannett Company now owns *The Tennessean*. Frank Sutherland, the current editor, says Gannett no longer permits its reporters to misrepresent themselves.

the disclosure of such deceptions unquestionably harms the public impression of journalism, both print and broadcast. The disclosure of undercover operations that are *not* so defensible further harms journalism's reputation. And public sentiment in some surveys already ranks the craft beneath "no opinion."

Does, therefore, underground reporting lose in public regard what it gains in public service? Is the deception worth the risk? These are two more questions journalists must sometimes answer without recourse to a set of rules or a code of ethics. As stated earlier, I don't believe such codes do, or ever can, cover all the cases that may arise or all the circumstances that may be involved.

CHAPTER 8

Competition

Being the city hall reporter for the *Winston-Salem Journal* was even more instructive than being the sports editor. The city's veteran mayor, Marshall Kurfees, was in the colorful tradition of southern showboat politicians, or at least he tried to be. One year, not untypically, he was reelected on the slogan, "Put the Jam on the Lower Shelf, Where the Little Man Can Reach It."

Kurfees, whose career ended later in a hopeless effort to defeat Senator Sam J. Ervin Jr., was regarded as at least a harmless mayor. It was well known, however, that slogan or no slogan, he was not the creature of "the little man" but mostly of the city's leading business figures. These made up a power structure that was not to be trifled with in the home city of Reynolds Tobacco, Wachovia Bank, Hanes Hosiery and even Goody's Headache Powder. Kurfees did little to buck this power structure, but toward the end of his third or maybe fourth term, word leaked through the city that its fathers had tired of the old mayor and wanted a new one. Marshall Kurfees was not to run again.

The mayor's office was on my regular beat, and though I had not long been covering him, Kurfees and I had developed a comfortable relationship. My counterpart, Gene Whitman, the veteran city hall reporter for the afternoon — and rival — *Twin City Sentinel,* was even closer to the mayor. Sometimes, Whitman and I would sit in Kurfees' office and chew the fat with him. Apparently, this was the mayor's favorite occupation, since the only work I remember him doing was taking an occasional phone call. Even that, as far as I ever saw, usually led only to more fat chewing.

When Kurfees was down to only a few weeks left in office, I had no reason to doubt that, having lost high-level favor, he was just time-serving. So I was stunned one afternoon to find a big headline across the top of page one in the *Sentinel:*

KURFEES SAYS HE'LL RUN AGAIN

The story, of course, was under the byline of Gene Whitman. It reported that leading citizens, or some such euphemism, had tried and failed to find another candidate and finally had decided to support Marshall Kurfees for another term. Locking the barn after the horse was stolen, I immediately confronted Kurfees and demanded to know why the story had been given to the *Sentinel*. The mayor lit a cigar, smiled benignly and said: "Gene promised me that big headline."

I could have guaranteed as big a headline, and the morning *Journal* had more circulation and clout than the afternoon *Sentinel*. But the real reason, I was sadly certain and still am, was that I had taken the *supposed* story for granted while my rival — an older and closer friend of the mayor — had kept on digging for the *real* story. Out of his long experience, Gene Whitman had figured all along that a suit- able replacement candidate would be hard to find. And I had been roundly scooped by the competition, as had my paper; it was a bitter potion for any reporter and one not likely to be forgotten.

This harsh lesson came not long before the great old *Herald-Tribune* in faraway New York City, though seemingly still in its glory days, began to slip toward its sad extinction. The *H-T* then appeared on the streets in New York every night at 9 p.m. while the first edition of *The New York Times* did not hit the newsstands until 9:15 p.m. So by 9:05 p.m., a *Times* "news clerk" — as the paper insisted on calling its copy boys — had raced to the *Times* building on West 43d Street with a copy of the *Herald-Tribune* on which the ink was scarcely dry.

Times editors then would pore over the competing *H-T* to see which of its stories or angles the *Times* did not have. There might be quite a few. Perhaps because *H-T* editors knew their paper was in financial danger, it was highly enterprising and had a daring staff compared to the "good, gray *Times*." As a result of the *Times* editors' nightly scrutiny of the *H-T* and the quick succession of orders they then would send out, the saying was born that "the *Times* is edited by the *Herald-Tribune*."[1]

Nowhere was this more nearly true than in the Washington bureau, where I worked after leaving Winston-Salem and Nashville. The cus-

---

[1] A more colorful saying was that "drink is the curse of the *Herald-Tribune* but women are the bane of the *Times*."

tom then was that most of the bureau staff, having done a day's work, would depart for home by 6 or 7 p.m. But each week it would be the turn of some reporter to work the copy desk at night until the final edition had been "put to bed" in New York, or until an editor had called to say a formal "good night."

On many such watches, the "late man" would have a lonely and uneventful vigil. Sometimes, however, news would break after the regular staff had called it a day. In other instances, some other newspaper (after the early sixties, more often a television network) would run a story that had not been covered in the *Times* or that had some angle the *Times* story did not include. Then it would be the late man's job to "match" that story or angle. This was not usually an easy task because news sources typically were asleep or out to dinner. Often, even when sources could be located, they were unwilling or unable to talk.

If the late man were the Pentagon reporter, moreover, he might know little about Democratic Party politics; or if he were a political reporter, he probably had no sources at the Pentagon.[2] It still would be his job either to match the competition's story or to appease demanding editors in New York. Neither was easy to do.

Once, while with the White House press on one of President Kennedy's weekend trips to Cape Cod, I was called out of my hotel-room bed by a *Times* editor, who informed me rather nastily that the Associated Press story about some political development took an approach different from my version.

"How, please?" the editor asked, which was *Times* jargon for "How could this happen?" or "What's your excuse?" The editor was suggesting, without actually saying so, that the AP story must be right, so mine must be wrong. But for once, I was able to silence him and return happily to bed.

"Don't worry about the AP," I said. "The AP's down in the bar, drunk."

Most of the time, however, a reporter getting such a call-back has little choice but to try to track down whatever the editor wants. Years ago, nothing inspired more nighttime calls to the Washington bureau and the unfortunate late-man-of-the-week than the appearance of the *Herald-Tribune's* first edition fifteen minutes before the *Times'* and the

---

[2] I use "he" and "man" in this context because in my time, I regret to say, only two women were on the Washington bureau's reporting staff of about 30. Today, probably about half the *Times* staff are women.

frantic scrutiny the *H-T* then received from *Times* editors in New York. And no one more frequently produced call-back stories that the Washington bureau was ordered to match than the late Marguerite Higgins.

For this reason, in the Washington bureau, the hour from 9 to 10 p.m. once was known, not fondly, as "the Maggie Higgins Hour." Ms. Higgins was an accomplished reporter with an extensive stable of sources. She could and did cover wars and revolutions abroad as well as political campaigns and social conflict at home, shaming and sometimes enraging many a male competitor. She was not regularly stationed in Washington but frequently wrote about events in the capital; so I and my colleagues had to chase down many a Higgins story, not all of which proved totally accurate.

Maggie Higgins was a good journalist and a tough competitor — and, not incidentally, a pioneer in the long-overdue breakthrough of women into what had been a mostly male preserve. I have recalled the Higgins hour here, however, not just in memory of an impressive colleague[3] but to question one of the shibboleths of journalism in which many editors, reporters and especially publishers have a virtually theological faith. Over the years, when I have previously, always gingerly, questioned journalists' faith in competition (a faith that I mostly share), I've invariably encountered shocked disapproval. But, gingerly, I'll try again.

As in free enterprise generally, it's relatively easy to make the case for competition in journalism. There's no question that more than one newspaper or broadcaster covering the same city or institution or government, or several reporters working the same beat for competing organizations, tends to produce more aggressive and inquisitive coverage. Working any area without competition can cause a reporter, a newspaper or a broadcaster to become complacent and sloppy, not to mention less hungry to be the best. (If unchallenged, you already are the best, by definition.) Nor is there competing work by which to measure one's own or to highlight one's errors of omission or commission.

In Winston-Salem, the *Journal* and the *Sentinel* were competitive — as I learned from Gene Whitman — but they were jointly owned by an overall corporation, the Piedmont Publishing Company. The *Journal* staff actually shared a newsroom with *Sentinel* reporters; they were on

---

[3] Ms. Higgins died of a rare disease contracted while, typically, she was reporting from Southeast Asia. She did perhaps her most celebrated work covering the Korean War.

the right-hand side of the big second-floor space, and we on the left, with an aisle and a vast human gulf down the middle.[4]

Each paper had its own copy desk, though they shared the same wire-service news tickers and sent copy in padded cylinders up the same old-fashioned compressed-air tubes to the same third-floor composing room. (In occasional nostalgic dreams, I still hear the hiss of those tubes and the "thock" of returning cylinders spurting out on the copy desk.) Despite this proximity, however, and the fact that advertisers had to buy space in both papers if they bought it in either, the vigorous competition between the two staffs was real and serious, though mostly good-natured.

Piedmont Publishing also owned WSJS-TV and radio, the NBC outlets and the city's premier broadcasters. Both papers were combined on Sundays into the *Journal and Sentinel,* a fat and profitable publication put together and edited by the *Journal* staff. The Federal Communications Commission now will not permit such a monopoly of news dissemination to be perpetuated in any community.[5] The rationale here, which is a good one, is that an unchallenged and less than public-spirited owner could manipulate, for political, economic or whatever reasons, the information available to a relatively helpless population. That's just too much noncompetitive power, even though the Winston-Salem version still left room for an aspiring reporter like me to be soundly beaten by a shrewd veteran.

After my time in Winston-Salem, Piedmont Publishing was sold to Media General of Richmond, Va., because the law required WSJS-TV and the radio station to be spun off in order to break the former monopoly. While working at the *Journal,* I had never observed Piedmont[6] to use its power invidiously. If anything, the company seemed to me to be a too-zealous promoter of the city, the state, and an amorphous brand of far-from-right-wing conservatism. Even that relatively benign attitude, however, might have been altered (for better or worse) had there been vigorous competition from another newspaper or broadcaster or both.

---

[4] *The Tennessean* and the *Banner* once had the same kind of joint ownership and shared the same building in Nashville. But the rivalry was far more intense than in Winston-Salem. When I worked at *The Tennessean,* the competition with the *Banner* was so severe that there was no connecting door inside the building. To get from one newsroom to the other, which few wanted to do, one had to walk out of *The Tennessean's* front door to the sidewalk and then reenter the *Banner's* front door.

[5] In 2000, the FCC unwisely began to reconsider this rule.

[6] The principal owner was Gordon Gray; he later became president of the University of North Carolina and then was a high official in the Eisenhower administration.

Unhappy developments, as I saw them, ultimately demonstrated to me what the absence of competition could mean. As a cost-saving measure, it was decided that the editorial-writing staffs and the sports departments of the morning *Journal* and the afternoon *Sentinel* should be combined. Why, it was reasoned, have two sports reporters covering, say, the Saturday afternoon Duke-Carolina football game when a single writer could attend and produce the necessary story for the combined Sunday edition? Why have two editorial writers specializing in local politics when one could write what needed to be written and the result could be published in either the morning or the afternoon paper?

In my judgment, then as well as in recall, the sports combination was not really a success, though it worked well enough administratively. But I thought coverage suffered because the sports reporter was the only person writing on each sports subject. For instance, if the reporter was writing about NASCAR (which began as a small auto-racing operation in the *Journal* circulation area) there was no local competition to keep him alert and aggressive. Furthermore, there was no competing yardstick by which to measure his work — or for him to measure himself.

He was also more vulnerable to pressure from NASCAR than two (or more) competing reporters would have been. One Christmas while I was sports editor of the *Journal,* NASCAR sent the sports department an expensive fruit basket and a case of whiskey. I sent both back, more in sorrow than in anger, and over staff protests.

The merger of the editorial writers seemed to cause less damage to editorial-page content, perhaps because the thinking involved in editorial writing does not need competition as much as reporting does. By the time of the merger, I had become an editorial writer myself, the two papers' specialist in foreign affairs. This was a bit of a joke since I was neither expert nor much interested in that field.

I didn't like the combined-staff arrangement but not because of lack of competition. My complaint was that I did not know on which editorial page my work would appear. As a *Journal* partisan, I resented occasionally being published in the *Sentinel,* and as a morning-newspaper buff I was convinced that the *Journal's* opinion page carried more weight in the community. I still think this kind of pride in one's work is a genuine morale factor.

In retrospect, however, I believe I also should have *wanted* a competing voice on foreign affairs. It would have been a useful challenge, causing me to think more seriously on the subject rather than too often reacting instinctively. The only editorial I wrote that was "spiked" (killed) was in opposition to the Eisenhower administration's armed intervention in Lebanon. The Winston-Salem newspapers generally supported that administration, but I remember sulking an entire morning over this "censorship."

Actually, it was nothing of the kind. Opinions differed on this early act of U.S. interventionism, as they still do when the United States intervenes today. My hot response probably would have been spiked as too hasty even before the editorial staffs were merged.

Obviously, however, if there was only one editorial staff for two papers, there could be no debate between the two on the Eisenhower administration, legalized liquor or anything else. Diversity of opinion unquestionably had been reduced. That fact was apparent to me and others at the time, and it is one reason many of us opposed combining the editorial-page staffs.

Although it's not so easy to make a case *against* competition, either in journalism specifically or in free enterprise generally, such arguments occasionally do need to be made. Competition usually results in a better mousetrap but it can also produce shoddy work, false claims, cut-throat practices and outright fraud.

Fraud can appear in journalism when reporters feel themselves dangerously challenged by a rival or are overly ambitious; they may be too anxious to get ahead and make a reputation, receive a promotion and a higher salary, or all of the above. These are conditions that can and often do afflict anyone in any line of work, but journalism tends to be more public than, say, banking or brokerage. Plagiarism or a deliberately faked story, if exposed, is more likely to be publicized — often by the perpetrator's own newspaper or broadcast outlet — than would an incident in which a businessperson undercut an in-house rival with a whispering campaign.

So when a Pulitzer Prize story turns out to be a fake, the world does not fail to hear about it. This, in fact, happened a few years ago to *The Washington Post,* which disclosed the fraud and fired the culprit. Nor can the matter be kept secret when a well-known local columnist is accused of being an occasional plagiarist. When this occurred in 1999, *The Boston Globe* did not even try to keep it secret but put out the story itself and fired the accused. Such incidents, however, seem to be relatively rare. (Of course, we don't know how often they may occur but are not discovered and punished.) But the greater problem in journalism, in my opinion, is not that of reporters or columnists unethically enhancing their work, as alleged in the preceding cases.

It lies rather in the competitive efforts of all news agencies, print or broadcast, to catch up when they've been momentarily outdone. When a reporter in any bureau is confronted at 10 p.m. or later with the dictum to match someone else's story, he or she may be able to find the necessary sources to get the job done properly if the reporter is able and experienced. But if no sources are quickly at hand, several unhappy possibilities exist:

- The reporter may tell the home office honestly that it's impossible to match the opposition story. Since this is not a course likely to improve a reporter's standing with his or her editors, it is not often followed.
- The reporter may find sources that know little more than he or she does but don't want to admit it, so the information from such sources can be incomplete, misleading or just plain wrong.
- With or without such uninformed sources, the reporter may rely on his or her own experience and background in order to concoct a response that, again, may be incomplete, misleading or just plain wrong.
- Even if the reporter can't confirm the opposition story, he or she may judge it to be correct and advise the editors to accept it without confirmation even though, to begin with, the story may have been incomplete, misleading or just plain wrong.
- The reporter may invent a response — usually a bogus confirmation — and hope for the best. The reporter may even get away with it.

All these possibilities, except the first, involve some degree of deception, and all are the direct consequence of competition. Had not some competitor come up with the story or the angle to be matched, which is not necessarily accurate, the reporter on the late watch could have continued to read a novel or watch television as usual, and no harm would have been done.

Editors bear considerable responsibility for such competitive pressure. All too often, what they want matched is not important or certain enough to risk the possibility of even mild deception. But editors are driven by competition to want everything in their newspaper or broadcast that may be in any competitor's, although they usually are reluctant to credit the other journal with discovering anything original.

For example, if *The Washington Post* or the *Chicago Tribune* has an exclusive story or quotation or explanation for an event, *The New York Times* will be reluctant either to ignore what these competitors have published or to absorb their exclusive into its own reporting, giving full credit for its origins. The *Post* and the *Tribune,* if the situation were reversed, would be equally reluctant.

To some extent the editors are right because somebody else's exclusive has not been confirmed by their own reporters (and may be incomplete, misleading or just plain wrong). The same editors, though, could state plainly and frankly that such-and-such was reported by a competitor but could not be immediately confirmed. Such a procedure would make the material available to their readers but warn them about its credibility and lay the onus on the competitor if the material does prove inaccurate.

This sensible course is not often followed, however, for — you guessed it — a competitive reason: Few publications or broadcasters want to give a competitor credit for having outdone them, even if the competitor's story is questionable.

Afternoon newspapers, most of which — owing to television — are now as extinct as Vesuvius, used to have a particular problem: the so-called second-day angle. Other than for natural disasters, which can happen at any time, news tends to break favorably for the morning cycle. Even in the heyday of afternoon papers, speeches, announcements and other events usually were timed for the morning cycle. This was the case because in most cities the morning paper was the most widely read and the most prestigious.[7] That meant the afternoon paper had to find some new angle on these same events since its stories would not appear until later.

Afternoon and wire-service reporters, therefore, had to be adept at writing "over-nighters" with a catchy second-day angle. These stories, which were written after their afternoon papers already had gone to press on one day, were intended for the next day's afternoon editions. Over-nighters had to tell afternoon readers something new about a story that already had appeared in the morning papers.

A morning-paper lead, for example, might read as follows:

President Clinton told the American people today that he had not had sexual relations with "that woman — Miss Lewinsky."

---

[7] Not always. St. Louis and Washington, D.C. (before the *Post* and the old *Times-Herald* joined forces), come to mind as cities in which afternoon papers once were dominant.

An over-night lead on the same story would mention a different angle:

> President Clinton risked impeachment yesterday if he should be found to have lied in telling the American people that he had not had sexual relations with Monica Lewinsky.

There's no factual quarrel with that hypothetical over-nighter. It could be considered, however, to have suggested the possibility of a presidential lie. It might also be regarded as having prematurely raised the possibility of impeachment. Over-nighters, which informed millions of afternoon readers for generations, presented at least two obvious dangers. One danger was that whatever might be borrowed from the morning-paper story, with too little opportunity for independent checking, might in some way be inaccurate. A second danger was that the search for a second-day angle might lead even reputable reporters to stretch their material — by untried theory, exaggeration, irrelevant background or, as in my hypothetical over-nighter, by inference.

The second danger for afternoon papers was enhanced by doubled competition, between afternoon papers themselves and between them and their morning counterparts. Afternoon editors and reporters typically sought to make up for not being first by being more exciting. That's why, with honorable exceptions, afternoon papers generally were considered racier than more sober morning journals.

That's also why the television-forced disappearance of most "pm's" is a two-edged development. Diversity of opinion and approach has been diminished, and too many one-newspaper towns have resulted[8] (though most have radio and TV, too, and many a morning newspaper now publishes around the clock). But the risks inherent in second-day stories and catch-up journalism also have been substantially reduced by the demise of so many afternoon papers.

Perhaps even more dangerous is the journalist's constant desire to be first with the news — to beat the competition.

How can that be bad? Doesn't it create alert, aggressive journalism, keep reporters and editors hungry, ward off complacency? If the

---

[8] The afternoon *Twin City Sentinel,* with which I and other morning *Journal* reporters competed in Winston-Salem, was a lamented victim of the trend, as was the *Nashville Banner.* The defunct *Washington Evening Star* once was the capital's leading newspaper, and deservedly so.

Times or any other news purveyor can claim to be consistently out front, or to be first in print or on the air with a particularly important story — the resignation of President Nixon to avoid impeachment in 1974 or the acquittal of the four New York policemen who killed Amadou Diallou in 1999 — isn't that good for public and professional prestige? Isn't it good for ratings and circulation, in-house ego and reader service?

Advocates of the free-enterprise theory certainly would answer "yes" (although newspaper circulation does not always respond quickly and certainly to competitive advantage). But the hitch is that being first is good only if those first reports are accurate. Being first with a clinker, as too often happens, does no one any good, least of all the guilty newspaper or broadcaster, and particularly if the story has to be retracted. It then becomes a public humiliation for journalism generally.

Even if a first story is correct on the main point but incomplete in details or explanation, it doesn't necessarily serve readers well. If some other publication or broadcaster provides a later but more detailed and comprehensive analysis of what happened and why — a better mousetrap — its prestige may get a bigger boost than the competitor that was first.

Beating the competition is particularly important to broadcasters since they can interrupt any regularly scheduled program, at any moment, with an important news bulletin. In contrast, even for the most cataclysmic event, modern newspapers usually must wait for the next edition, which may be hours in the future. President Kennedy was murdered in the middle of the day on Nov. 22, 1963; *The New York Times* did not report even that monumental news until its regular first edition appeared at 9:15 p.m.

The popular image of urchins on the street shouting "Extra!" to signal a big story belongs to the era of Horatio Alger; it has not been part of the American scene since the rise of broadcasting. No newspaper today can get out an Extra, no matter how earth-shaking the story, in time to beat radio and television bulletins. Few even try. In my *New York Times* office, on days when I had reason to anticipate some important news break, I used to keep a television set tuned to the Cable News Network, with the sound turned off.

Still, it's hard to see how NBC News (I'm using that excellent organization only for another hypothetical example) has performed an important public service because its anchor got on the air with news of an important political development perhaps a few minutes or just a few seconds ahead of CBS or ABC News. Being first gives a network bragging rights and will certainly earn its news department plaudits in the executive chamber — maybe even a raise for the responsible correspondent.

What, however, did those few extra minutes or seconds mean to the viewing public? Soon enough, they were going to learn the news from the other networks or, belatedly, from a newspaper. Someday, perhaps, they would learn the news even earlier from the Internet. (I'm not talking here about the kind of exclusive story known only to one news agency.) And what if NBC News (again used only for example) put out a misleading or incomplete first report that was soon topped in accuracy or comprehensiveness or both by one of the other networks? In this case, being first might actually have damaged NBC's viewers as well as its reputation. A Pyrrhic victory indeed!

Therefore, competition, while certainly at the heart of the most alert and useful journalism, should not always be the supreme value, especially when it causes a loss of accuracy or completeness. Excessive competitive spirit, like uncontrolled ambition, can be too much of what is basically a good thing.

A remark by Ben Bradlee, when he was the great managing editor of *The Washington Post,* seems to me apropos. Asked to compare the *Post* and *The New York Times,* Bradlee gave high marks to both but reverted to his Navy days to say of the *Times:* "I like its cruising speed."

I take that to have meant that he admired the day-in, day-out, sometimes first, sometimes not, but usually accurate and comprehensive performance of a major competitor. By that definition, developing a good "cruising speed" seems to me what newspapers and broadcasters alike should strive for, rather than putting so much emphasis on beating or matching the competition.

Closely related to competitive excellence is the question of whether the reading or viewing public is best served by a capable general reporter or by a knowledgeable specialist.

When I was Washington bureau chief for *The New York Times,* I never found a satisfactory answer to that question. Neither, so far as I know, did my predecessor, James Reston, nor my successor, Max Frankel, nor any of *his* successors. Of necessity, we only coped as best we could with a difficult problem.

To be specific: What should be done when, say, the Defense Department appropriation is being considered in a committee of Congress or being debated on the House or Senate floor? Should the assignment desk entrust the coverage to an experienced congressional reporter? (This is a reporter who's learned that you can cover the House of Representatives by knowing maybe 10 of its 435 members but who also knows that the trick is to find out which 10.) Or should an experienced Pentagon reporter be called upon?

If the job goes to the congressional expert, he or she might not know where the bodies are buried — or the pork is hidden — in the intricate, multibillion-dollar defense budget. Such a reporter might not know the arguments for and against a new fighter plane, or another aircraft carrier for the Atlantic fleet, and might perhaps be basically ignorant of a bureaucratic conflict on budgetary matters between the Joint Chiefs of Staff and the secretary of defense. Or maybe the congressional expert is a neophyte in something like the recent debate over an antimissile defense and a possible U.S. breakout from the ABM Treaty with the former Soviet Union.

So is the preferable alternative to call on an experienced Defense Department reporter? Someone who can find his or her way through the Pentagon labyrinth might not be able, as Lyndon Johnson once said of Robert McNamara, to "find his ass with both hands" on Capitol Hill. Would a Defense Department reporter know the most important figures on the relevant committees, who are not always the chairpersons or the ranking minority members? Such a reporter probably wouldn't have trusted sources among congressional staff, who can be a fount of information on members and politics. Nor might such a reporter even fully understand arcane congressional procedures and prerogatives. And though the Pentagon expert certainly would know the defense budget, would he or she realize all that could be done to it cleverly, sometimes secretly, in committee markup.

The Pentagon specialist would not necessarily know which members of the House or Senate drank too much, talked too much, had earned colleagues' animosity and distrust (or their respect), were or weren't in special hock to interests or lobbyists or other members, or neglected their homework or their wives. Such information might be irrelevant to the defense budget but not to those debating or reporting on it.

Furthermore, influential members of Congress might not want to cooperate with a Pentagon expert they don't know, but they'd happily take advantage of a friendly congressional reporter largely ignorant of defense matters. And since the latter would have no confidential sources "across the river" in the Pentagon, the congressional reporter might be easy prey to the military's designated spokesperson.

It doesn't really solve the problem to ask both the Pentagon expert and the congressional whiz to do the job together. Most news agencies don't have enough reporters to do that. Even if they do, personalities have to be taken into account: Most beat reporters won't welcome an outsider invading their turf, and they might not even be willing to help such an outsider.

If that problem doesn't apply, a tandem, like a bicycle built for two, still is more unwieldy than a singleton. Who'll get the bigger byline? Who'll take the responsibility of leading, as well as the blame, if the duo gets scooped? And will important sources be more willing to deal confidentially with two reporters than with the one to whom they're accustomed?

In short, what course best serves the reader or viewer? The same question will arise on any specialized matter spilling over into more general politics, if it's an important story — say, a debate on atomic energy, or genetics or on the mushrooming complexities of health-care coverage.

Will a specialist in the subject matter do a better job *for the public* than a generalist on politics and process?

Though in recent years newspapers and broadcasters have turned more frequently to specialists — trained experts on the law, science, medicine, the environment, cyberspace — they still rely primarily on the generalist reporter working a particular beat.

An experienced reporter is assigned to, say, the Department of Justice, city hall, the Pentagon, the police department, the legislature, the local chamber of commerce — to some coherent segment of the overall coverage — to report anything important or interesting that happens in that area. In most cases, he or she is not an expert on anything, except covering a story (if that).

For years, James Reston hired young reporters to work in the Washington bureau of the *Times*[9] and went through the protocol of assigning them to cover the regulatory agencies: the numerous federal agencies that regulate the stock market, broadcasting, railroad rates,

---

[9] Reston hired reporters mostly by instinct rather than by exhaustive inquiry and interviewing. Judging applicants "by the seat of his pants," Reston probably brought more good journalists to the bureau and the *Times* than anyone of his era.

trucking, labor practices and a variety of other matters. When I joined the *Times* from the Nashville *Tennessean,* old hands in the bureau were snickering over a full-page ad in *Editor & Publisher* that listed me and other bureau reporters with the beats to which we had been assigned. Tom Wicker, the world was informed (to his dismay), covered the regulatory agencies.

I never did cover those agencies, not for a single day, and neither did any other reporter to whom Reston tried to give the job. The reason was plain: Although the regulatory agencies all were empowered by Congress to regulate something, that was their only unifying thread. They did not make up a coherent beat. They weren't even housed under one roof, like the Department of Justice, or in adjacent buildings, like the Department of Agriculture.

On my first day in the bureau, Wallace Carroll, the assistant chief, sent me to Capitol Hill to write about Congress (not a very coherent beat, either). Thus serendipitously, I became a political reporter, mercifully far removed from the regulatory agencies.[10] The net result of Reston's efforts, in my time and still, is usually that when one of those agencies does something newsworthy — an occasional event in a humdrum daily process — whatever bureau reporter has free time is dispatched to write it up.

The perpetually unresolved dilemma over specialists and reporters on beats, and my escape from the regulatory agencies, tell something useful about the beat system: No arrangement of beats ever devised can cover everything. Should the old Atomic Energy Commission (now the Nuclear Regulatory Commission), for instance, have fallen under the aegis of a science reporter or, since it makes bombs, a defense expert? (The AEC might even be considered a regulatory agency.)

In my view, however, the major problem with the beat system is that those assigned to a particular beat generally learn what they know about the subject or subjects they're supposed to write about *from the sources they develop.* This problem is fading, but only slightly, as specialists who know their subject academically (a law school graduate) or from personal involvement (a practicing doctor) are being drawn more often into journalism.

---

[10] I did do a short stint covering the Agriculture Department, perhaps because as a Southerner I was erroneously supposed to understand farming. This assignment ended abruptly when I referred in my first story to "bushels of cotton."

Most beats, however, still are covered by generalist reporters who begin with little or no independent knowledge, academic or otherwise, of the subjects they write about. Such a reporter, if assigned to cover the Treasury in Washington or the Department of Revenue in a state capital, must necessarily learn a lot of economics. But that's the rub: The reporter learns economics from the economists and bureaucrats making up the beat, the very people he or she is covering. Inevitably, the reporter's knowledge is colored by the sources from which it was derived.

There need be nothing dishonest about this process on the part of either the source or the reporter. The source wants the reporter — ultimately the public — to understand what's being done, why, and what are the presumed consequences. The reporter wants the source to explain to him or her — again, ultimately to the public — those very acts and that reasoning, both of which may be arcane. At best, both need and serve the other.

It rarely happens, however, nor should it be expected (except in the unusual cases of dissidents and whistle-blowers), that a source will argue against a policy of his or her agency or denigrate the steps being taken to follow it. Nor is a source likely to predict disaster or poor results, even though they may be possible consequences. He or she will almost certainly have an *economic* attitude that may be consciously or unconsciously imparted, along with more specific information, to the reporter. It's likely also that the source will demonstrate a *political* attitude.

Here, then, is a mentor — the source — with something like a blank slate — the reporter — to inscribe. Even if the source deals honorably with the reporter, the latter's views are likely to be influenced by those of the source. In turn, those views will have at least a subliminal (perhaps stronger) effect on the stories the reporter writes or broadcasts. And if the source should try to influence the reporter — the more political the source, the likelier such an effort — the effect may be even stronger, on the reader or viewer as well as on the reporter.

The obvious remedy for such a possibly one-sided education is more independently informed reporters. These persons have learned (in addition to their journalism skills) something about the subject matter they're writing about, perhaps from law or medical or business school, from assiduous reading, or from an earlier career in the armed forces or in criminal justice.

That, however, is an ideal. Journalism is not a widely admired craft, its practitioners are not often in high income brackets, and most specialists can achieve better financial and social status by practicing their specialty rather than by writing about it. Minorities, too, in this day of multicultural pressures, can earn more money and respect in almost any profession other than journalism.

So even though more independent authorities are now a part of print and broadcast news staffs, those staffs still lack expertise. This fact brings us back, of course, to that question to which I never found a satisfactory answer for the *Times* Washington bureau:

Is the public better served by the specialist who knows a lot about one thing or by the generalist who knows a little about a lot of things? Both, obviously, are needed. But so far, the answer from journalism remains — largely by tradition and default — the generalist.

CHAPTER 9

Snapshots

On Nov. 2, 1948, recently turned 21 years of age and my mind made up, I entered a polling booth in Southern Pines, N.C. I was going to cast my first vote for Thomas E. Dewey, Republican, for president of the United States.

That may startle readers of the articles I wrote years later in *The New York Times*. They probably think of me as a Democrat — and a liberal Democrat at that. They'd be right, too. But 1948 was more than a half-century ago.

I had not then been long returned to civilian life from my first hitch in the U.S. Navy, where I had been last stationed at Tacoma, Wash.[1] There, while typically goofing off one day in 1946 from my assigned job as a yeoman, I had listened on radio as President Harry S Truman addressed Congress. In his usual blunt fashion, he said he was going to draft into the armed forces the railroad workers who were then staging one of the nationwide strikes of the post-World War II years.

My father, a veteran conductor for the Seaboard Air Line Railroad (now several mergers in the corporate past), was one of those striking workers. He was hale and hearty but too old to be drafted. Because I revered my father, on the spot I made up my mind about Truman. I swore to myself: I'll *never* vote for that little S.O.B.

The end of the strike caused the president, but not me, to relent. In 1948 I was still determined to vote against him even though his opponent turned out to be Governor Dewey of New York, forever identified by Alice Roosevelt Longworth as "the little man on the wedding cake." In those pre-voting-machine days, I actually had the pencil in my hand to mark my ballot for Dewey.

I was not only the son of a railroad man, however. I was the youngest member of a family of yellow-dog Democrats.

---

[1] As a reservist, I was called back to duty in 1952, during the Korean War.

Ah, hell, I thought. I can't cast my first vote for a Republican. Besides, the polls say Dewey's sure to win, so it won't make any difference if I vote for that little S.O.B.[2]

More than 50 years later, I'm convinced that millions of Americans, as certain as I was that Harry Truman was a lost cause, did just what I did on that historic Election Day. Because Americans hate to vote for a loser, they entered the booth resigned to supporting Dewey, a man they didn't much like. But when the pencil hovered over the ballot, they couldn't do it. They cast instead what they thought was a hopeless ballot, one that wouldn't matter anyway, for Truman.

History records, therefore, that the biggest upset in presidential history was won by that little S.O.B. who had wanted to draft my father into the Army.

1948, of course, and 1936 — when the *Literary Digest* poll predicted that Governor Alfred M. Landon, Republican of Kansas, would defeat Franklin D. Roosevelt — are cautionary years in the history of presidential opinion surveys. Alf Landon carried only Maine and Vermont, so whatever doubts still exist about the scientific nature and accuracy of polls are almost always expressed in accounts of the 1936 and 1948 elections.

Indeed, the polling methodology that predicted those two elections was seriously flawed, though in different ways. In 1936, for instance, the *Literary Digest* actually conducted only a *straw poll,* a procedure then commonplace but now regarded as inadequate.

The *Digest* distributed 10 million ballots, seemingly a huge sampling, but the ballots were sent only to households with telephone numbers in a directory or with automobiles registered by their states. In the Depression year 1936, few people other than the well-to-do had either a phone or an auto. Though the *Digest* received more than 2 million completed ballots, which was a decent return of 20 percent of those sent out, the results were so badly skewed by the original procedure that the predicted Landon vote, a winning 57 percent, was overstated by 19 percentage points. The Crossley, Roper and Gallup polls, using methodology more similar to today's, correctly foretold FDR's immense victory. The *Literary Digest* disappeared.

Twelve years later, in 1948, the more "scientific" polls had their day of humiliation. Roper stopped polling in September and last

---

[2] I'm glad I also voted that day for W. Kerr Scott for governor of North Carolina, whom I later wrote about when he was a U.S. senator.

reported that Dewey had a 15-point lead. And he may, indeed, have had such a lead then. Gallup and Crossley kept at it longer, but not long enough; both predicted a five-point Dewey victory.

Harry Truman seemed to be shouting down a rain barrel when he cited, in Ohio, the "one big poll that counts — that is the voice of the American people speaking at the ballot box." The press, however, was persuaded by the other, published polls. Drew Pearson wrote a column analyzing Dewey's new White House staff. Walter Lippmann, Marquis Childs, the Alsop brothers — all influential columnists of that era — were just as confident of a Dewey victory. So were *The New York Times, The Wall Street Journal, Time* and *Life.* In a *Newsweek* survey of 50 respected political writers, not one predicted that Truman would win. Clark Clifford, Truman's aide, was so depressed by the *Newsweek* poll that he tried to hide it from the president.

Only big page-one headlines all across the nation, most of which quoted Truman's speeches, even suggested that a contest was going on. Like Dewey and the columnists, editorial writers thought it was all over before the voting.

As it turned out in the four-way race (Henry Wallace, Progressive, and Strom Thurmond, Dixiecrat, were also on the ballot), Truman handily carried the popular count and won 303 electoral votes. Post-election analyses showed that not only had the poll-takers stopped work too soon; they also had too many high-income Republicans in their samples. Furthermore, they had no reliable methods of determining which respondents actually would vote or of dealing with the undecideds. The latter were an important factor in a year in which the Truman trend developed late (in my case, at the last possible minute).

That trend obviously led to the president's reelection and to the historic events of Truman's second term.[3] It also pointed up what is probably the most profound single conclusion about polls to be drawn from *any* election: The result of the best, most careful opinion survey is only a snapshot, a measure of opinion at the time the poll is taken. That snapshot may not be accurate tomorrow or next week or on some future Election Day.

Nevertheless, later in November 1948, the National Opinion Research Center at the University of Chicago found that despite Truman's unpredicted victory, most of the public still trusted the polls. Since then, moreover, poll-takers have worked assiduously to elimi-

---

[3] For instance, his decision to enter the Korean War in 1950 and his later firing of General Douglas MacArthur.

nate or compensate for that year's flawed methodology. Judging by the results, they've largely succeeded; national elections since 1948 have vindicated most poll predictions. So, in general, have state and local contests, though there have been some glaring exceptions.

A half-century after Harry Truman gloatingly displayed that famous 1948 *Chicago Tribune* headline — DEWEY DEFEATS TRUMAN — polls have a more prominent place than ever in American politics and therefore in the American press. Or is it vice versa?

Much, perhaps most, political coverage today is based on poll results. Major news organizations like *The Wall Street Journal,* CNN, *The New York Times* and the television network news departments sponsor closely watched and influential national samplings of public opinion. In virtually every state and city, local organizations — often primarily engaged in news coverage — provide polls of election prospects.

On a major election or primary day (say, in New Hampshire in a presidential year), the networks sponsor "exit polls" of voters coming out of the booth. Voters are asked: How did you vote, and why? The results enable network analysts to tell the public, almost as soon as the voting ends, who has won and even by how much, and sometimes why. Exit-poll predictions are so seldom wrong,[4] or even off by a big margin, that viewers wait breathlessly and confidently not for final returns — which may be hours or days away — but for a network "call."[5]

Of course, what NASA likes to call "anomalies" do sometimes occur in modern polling. In late February 2000, for example, polls showed Vice President Al Gore ahead in the New Hampshire Democratic primary by about 12 points. At the same time, John McCain had an eight-point lead over George W. Bush in the Republican primary. On March 7, however, McCain won a huge victory by 19 points, and Gore defeated Bill Bradley by somewhat more than 12. So were the polls wrong, as a number of critics were eager to suggest?

Not really. The winners had been properly predicted, which is the main objective, even though the magnitude of victory in both primaries was off. But even there, poll-takers could cite a plausible reason: the

[4] They did lead to network — hence public — confusion about who had won Florida in the 2000 presidential election. Ultimately, George W. Bush won, though some network "calls" had seemed to give the state to Al Gore.
[5] If one network should correctly "call" an election or a primary for one candidate or another, even as little as a minute before a competing broadcaster, the winning network may well boast the next day in full-page ads: "First to call New Hampshire!" What that network actually has gained over its competition, if anything other than bragging rights, cannot be so concisely expressed.

difficulty of predicting the behavior of independent voters, especially when, as in New Hampshire, they could vote in either primary (but not both). Many independents would not say ahead of time which primary they would enter; some didn't want to commit themselves, and some genuinely had not made up their minds. Poll analysts were forced to make reasonable decisions, based on past performance and other plausible factors, as to how New Hampshire's independents would behave on primary day.

When it arrived, independent voters broke far more heavily than had been logically expected in favor of the Republican primary, which meant more independent votes for McCain and fewer for Gore's opponent, Bill Bradley. Both victors therefore won more easily than had been predicted; in the Democratic case, the entire primary campaign in all states may have been decided, as an incipient Bradley bubble, already leaking, was deflated in New Hampshire. Thus, the New Hampshire poll figures were not wrong but reflected the difficulty of predicting the behavior of uncommitted voters.

Polls can affect more than the actual race they predict. In national elections, for instance, the results of Eastern-state voting, if broadcast before polls close in voting places in the West, can have a significant effect on Western voters. Polls can even influence the *next* election. If, for instance, a candidate is found to have fared badly in a particular state or with a certain segment of voters, such as women, blacks or Roman Catholics, a successor candidate may campaign vigorously for that constituency in the next election — or perhaps write it off altogether.

If taken early enough, surveys also can scare off politicians who might otherwise contest or even win an election. In 1999, for instance, polls showing Hillary Clinton a heavy favorite for a Democratic Senate nomination in New York cleared the field of other persons who might have entered the race. The first President Bush had scored so heavily in post-Gulf War popularity polls that numerous Democratic possibilities backed away from challenging him in 1992, probably opening the way for the less-well-known governor of Arkansas, Bill Clinton, to take the Democratic nomination and win the presidency.

It can work the other way, too. Surveys may indicate that it would be unwise for a candidate to put time and resources into a particular state or to court a particular population group at the expense of others. On just such a basis in 1992, Bush all but conceded California to Clinton and the Democrats, perhaps fatally.

Perhaps more significantly, what polls tell candidates about the public popularity of, or disdain for, certain issues and actions will heavily influence how they treat those matters, pro or con. Many pro-choice candidates today once fervently opposed abortion, only to change with public opinion as reflected in polls. Similarly, few candidates today advocate the kinds of federal programs popular in the New Deal era of Franklin D. Roosevelt.

Fund-raising obviously is strongly affected by poll standings. In 2000, at a $25,000-per-couple party in Beverly Hills, Calif. — usually a money tree for Democratic candidates — a "top Democratic fund-raiser" told presidential candidate Al Gore that he had a "tough act to follow" in Bill Clinton. But, the moneyman added, "poll numbers help a lot. When polls show you're going to win, it's a lot easier" to raise campaign funds.[6]

Taken altogether, what the polls say heavily influences American politics in a variety of ways; and what the polls say is generally propagated, often magnified, by the press. Who would know who's ahead or likely to win, and sometimes what that information "means," if it weren't for headlines and news bulletins about the findings of Gallup, Mervyn Field, Peter Hart and other poll-takers? Who really persuaded the public that Tom Dewey was as good as elected in 1948? The polls or the press, the chicken or the egg?

Often, indeed, the press gives the public not just raw polling figures but the most widely accepted interpretation of what the polls say. Therefore, reporters and editors should know as much about polling, its strengths and weaknesses, its methodology and integrity, as they do about a candidate's record in public office, or the state of the Social Security system, or the flourishing (or lagging) economy of a particular state.

They should. But generally speaking, they don't.

George Gallup likes to tell a story about an elderly woman in one of his lecture audiences who rose to complain that she had never been polled. She should understand, he replied, that any individual's chance of being polled, in a population of more than 200 million, was no greater than that person's chance of being struck by lightning.

The lady replied: "But I *have* been struck by lightning."

---

[6] *The New York Times,* April 17, 2000, p. A16, column 3.

It's obvious that the more populous the constituency or city or state being surveyed, the smaller the chance that all its population can be polled. In a national poll, that chance is near nil. Hence, poll-takers use sampling, which is subject to error no matter how honestly, carefully and scientifically a poll is conducted. The immutable laws of chance (flip a coin and there's a 50 percent chance it'll come up "heads" and the same chance it'll come down "tails") mean that one poll out of 20, even if all are impeccably conducted, will be skewed by sampling error.

Sampling error is not a matter of someone making a mistake, although of course mistakes happen. It results from random chance (like being struck by lightning), from which there is no human escape. For this reason, the possibility of sampling error occurring must always be reported by those who make and publicize a survey.

If a sample is constructed to represent honestly a population of 100,000, about 1,060 persons will have to be included to keep the sample within what a newspaper reporting the poll results will call "a margin of error of plus-or-minus three points." Such a sample would represent barely more than 1 percent of the population being surveyed, so it would be easy to be slightly in error in compiling the sample. In fact, it would be all but impossible *not* to be.

For samples of different sizes, but of the same size population, statisticians have developed a method (too technical to be described here, even if I fully understood it) to measure the variation that minor deviations may cause in sample results as compared with the results that would have been obtained in an accurate census of the whole population. This is what is called the "margin of error," which is usually plus-or-minus three percentage points. The margin of error tells the public that "the chances are 95 out of 100, or better, that the results of this survey are within three percentage points of the results [that would have been obtained] if a census [of the whole population] had been taken using the same method."[7]

Or, put another way, there's one chance in 20 (five out of a hundred) that the margin of error is outside the range of plus-or-minus three percentage points.

Thus, if sample results show that respondents favor Candidate A by 45 percent, A will be favored by 42 percent to 48 percent of the

---

[7] Sheldon R. Gawiser and G. Evans Witt, *A Journalist's Guide to Opinion Polls* (Westport, Conn.: Praeger Publishers, 1994), pp. 86–8.

whole population at least 95 times in a hundred censuses. And this plus-or-minus 3 percent margin of error must be applied to *every* figure reported for the sample. It would apply, for instance, to the number of those who say they're likely to vote, or who are undecided, as well as to the number favoring a particular candidate.

Sampling error, if honestly calculated and presented, is not considered a major problem by poll-takers. Broadcast media, though, have a difficult time explaining to their audiences exactly what the margin of error reflects in a given poll. Television reports of opinion surveys, therefore, must be doubly guarded in the way they're presented, and the audience must be doubly cautious in receiving them.

Sampling error, however, is usually insignificant in comparison to the wording of survey questions. Wording — *what* is being asked — often has a direct impact on the answer. Clearly, the same respondents might give different responses to these questions:

- Do you favor a tax increase to raise the salaries of government bureaucrats?
- Do you favor a tax increase to meet necessary national needs, such as building highways and punishing criminals?
- Do you favor a tax increase if it's not necessary?

The problem is that even "advocacy" poll-takers — those who deliberately seek a predetermined outcome — seldom pose such obviously loaded queries. Even leading questions usually are more subtle than these. Nor are all advocacy poll-takers *necessarily* dishonest (overly partisan or strongly ideological might describe many).

A good survey question should be neutral in wording and designed to elicit not a desired answer but the unbiased opinion of the respondent. The same question must be asked in the same way of hundreds, perhaps thousands, of respondents, which is why most poll interviewers read their questions without variation in the wording. Even different words meaning much the same thing can affect results.

Public Opinion Quarterly has reported a study[8] in which respondents regarded the words *acceptable* [to you] and [do you] *favor* as virtually interchangeable, but an average of 30 percent of them found significant differences between these usages and [do you] *support*.

---

[8] Spring 1989 issue.

The original survey had used *acceptable* only. Press accounts of the survey, however, reported *acceptable, favor,* and *support* as if they were the same. There was no journalistic dishonesty here, but a flawed public understanding occurred nevertheless.

Questions, of course, must be understandable. They should be clear, balanced as between contrary positions, and direct and to the point. ("Do you like Clinton?" and "Do you approve of the job Clinton is doing?" are different questions.) If there's one way in which polls can be most easily misused for fraudulent propaganda purposes, it's probably by slippery wording. Even the sequence of questions can affect the answers. The first question in a series, for instance, may get the most considered response, and the last question may get the least. Or, if the answer to an early question is unfavorable to a candidate, a respondent may not support that candidate in reply to a later question. The respondent might have backed that candidate had it not been for that unfavorable earlier reply.

In 1978, the reliable political reporter Jim Perry of *The Wall Street Journal* went to South Carolina to report on a Senate race between Strom Thurmond, the venerable (even then) incumbent Republican, and Charles "Pug" Ravenel, a young Democrat. The Thurmond camp confided to Perry a pre-election poll purporting to show Thurmond far in the lead — suspiciously far, in Perry's experienced judgment.

Perry consulted the (usually Democratic) opinion researcher Peter Hart and was advised to ask to see the questions as well as the results. When Perry did, he found that a long series of queries about Thurmond and Ravenel had been so sequenced as to lead a respondent almost inevitably to the conclusion that any decent, right-minded American should vote for Strom Thurmond. The poll figures were not literally misrepresented, but they had been arrived at by calculated means. Though Perry properly ignored that particular poll, Thurmond won anyway (in 1978 in South Carolina, it would have been easier to beat George Washington than "Old Strom" — and it still may be).

Suppose, however, that the reported Thurmond lead had been more plausible, though still arrived at by a deliberate ranking of questions. Even an honest reporter might not have been suspicious enough to demand to see the entire survey rather than just the favorable result. On the other hand, if a poll shows a candidate ahead by, say, a ratio of 7 or 8 to 1, what was the use of taking a poll in such a lopsided situation? For propaganda?

The cardinal rule of poll reporting is, or should be: Always review the questions asked and tell the reader if they're too pointed or in "leading" order. And if the survey looks "loaded" one way or another — Peter Hart estimates that as many as 20 percent of surveys are advocacy polls — don't report it at all.

Here may arise another of those questions journalists must decide for themselves on the basis of experience and knowledge (in this case of survey techniques). Is this particular poll worth reporting? Or is it biased and questionable enough that honest journalism requires it to be spiked? Codes of ethics won't give you that answer, and whatever you decide, you're likely to be criticized by one side or the other as partisan, liberal, conservative, dishonest or easily conned.[9]

Weighting can be another source of skew in otherwise reputable polls. Weighting consists of assigning to a sample the proper percentage of a certain cohort, such as blacks or Jews or blue-collar workers, to represent the proportion of that segment in the population to be surveyed. A properly weighted sample is put together from a variety of sources: accepted demographics (as in census figures), a poll-taker's own surveys, exit polls, turnout records from previous elections.

A major problem with even a properly weighted election sample, however, is whether those included actually will vote. If a segment of a sample, or any significant part of that segment, stays home on Election Day, even careful weighting is wasted. Respondents usually answer quickly and truthfully about *who* they plan to vote for and then stick to it. But when respondents are asked *whether* they'll vote, an accurate answer is less easy to come by or to trust. When asked if they are registered to vote, for instance, 85 percent of Americans say they are. Actual registration figures for mid-2000 showed that, in fact, only 76 percent were on the voting rolls.

Therefore, poll-takers always ask a series of questions designed to zero in on a respondent's real intention. Unfortunately, such an intent, even if honest when expressed, can change in a day, a week or at the last minute (remember my oath never to vote for that little S.O.B.).

The respondent may not have lied about his or her intention (although some do). But he or she owes no fealty to the poll-taker and may have an honest change of mind. The campaign may disappoint, discourage or even disgust some persons. The kids may be sick on

---

[9] I once predicted, on what I should have known better than to consider good information, that a presidential election in Texas would be close. It wasn't. Those who had gulled me had a good laugh at my expense—the only laugh they got out of a landslide defeat.

Election Day. The car might not start. The weather may be miserable. Any number of things can transform an intent to vote into a decision to stay at home. And since many such happenings are unpredictable even to the respondent, he or she is more likely, even with no intent to deceive, to inflate rather than discount the probability that he or she will vote — a serious variable in poll-taking.

In a celebrated incident, the Harris organization in its final 1968 presidential poll showed the underdog Democratic candidate, Hubert H. Humphrey, finally pulling ahead of the Republican, Richard Nixon, by one point. Humphrey had trailed by declining margins since September. Gallup, in his final survey, still had Nixon ahead.

Did Lou Harris reflect Democratic leanings? If so, it was within permissible limits. On the basis of long experience, Harris decided that of respondents who seemed less likely to vote, a certain percentage in the end would go for the Democratic candidate (as had happened in earlier elections). Gallup did not interpret his figures, which were much the same as Harris', in the same way. Harris proved honestly wrong, Gallup proved honestly right, and Nixon was narrowly elected.

(The presence on the 1968 ballot of the segregationist George Wallace, a strong third-party candidate, may have helped bring about a different outcome from the one Harris thought he had reason to expect.)

Another potential source of polling error — stopping too soon — is well remembered from the Truman-Dewey election. Having had to swallow that bitter pill, poll-takers now keep surveying opinion right up to and sometimes on Election Day (as Harris and Gallup did in 1968, for instance). Still, as Peter Hart insists, polling failures usually result because "we're always learning the same lessons over again."[10]

He remembers painfully that in 1978 one of his clients, Democratic Senator Dick Clark of Iowa, an informal fellow who wore blue jeans in the Senate chamber, was leading his race for reelection by 62 percent to 26 percent in October. At that point, the Clark campaign virtually shut down (who wouldn't have?). But his opponent, in Hart's phrase, "pulled out all stops" in the last month and won 51 percent to 49 percent!

In contrast to 1936, the Depression year I mentioned earlier, about 95 percent of households in any given state have a telephone today. So random direct dialing, in which phone numbers in a selected area code

---

[10] In an interview with the author on April 7, 2000.

are called at random (to bypass unlisted numbers), is both the fastest and the least costly method of surveying. The area code is selected on the basis of past voting results, turnout and other such indicative data.

Here is an example of what may happen in such a telephone survey (numbers have been rounded off for simplicity):

1,000	calls are made
300	business firms answer and are not counted
500	nonworking phones or no-answers
200	valid households are reached, but
120	(60 percent) will not respond for a variety of reasons

So there are 80 valid responses, only 8 percent of the original 1,000 calls. But as Peter Hart and most poll-takers calculate, that's 40 percent of the 200 households actually reached, and that's the percentage of respondents poll-takers report.

To those 80 responding households, however, one more test has to be applied: Which resident is to be questioned?

If it's the person who just answered the phone, the sample is likely to rely too heavily on teenagers. To avoid such an imbalance, adept interviewers follow predetermined procedures to select the best-prepared household member actually to be surveyed.

To conduct random-dialing surveys, Hart has had a "telephone shop" in Akron, Ohio, since 1990, and 76 of the first 90 interviewers he hired are still working the phones there. To make a thousand-call survey, such as the one described, about 500 interviewers would work for roughly five hours. Actual interviews take only about 20 minutes each, but it may well take twice that long to find and question one respondent.

Those householders who hang up on the interviewer, or who refuse to respond, may do so for many reasons: irritation at being bothered again in an era of telemarketing, reluctance to get involved, fear of being identified politically or socially, disbelief in polls, worry that one's views will be considered irresponsible or ignorant. For whatever reasons, nonrespondents are a fact of life for which the reputable poll-taker must allow.

Nationally prominent poll sponsors, say, for an NBC/*Wall Street Journal* poll, have fewer problems with nonrespondents. Apparently, those called to take part in such a poll fancy themselves as being part of a "show" or a big media exposition, or just a major survey that matters.[11] Callers inquiring about local or state elections encounter greater resistance. Nonresponse is most prevalent when interviewers ask questions about a commercial product.

A severe problem, in addition to those nonrespondents, is the so-called socially responsible reply. One example might be a woman who doesn't want to admit that she's pro-life for fear of being regarded as out of step with her sex. A famous example occurred in the election of Douglas Wilder as the first black governor of Virginia. A Democrat, Wilder had a high level of support in a poll taken just before the voting. When the returns came in, however, he won by only a small margin. Many white Virginians apparently had not wanted to admit to a poll-taker that they would vote against a black candidate.

The best, though not infallible, way to guard against a socially acceptable response is to anticipate it. Poll-takers know, for example, that if a male interviewer asks a woman about women's issues (abortion, sexual abuse and so forth), he may well get different answers from those that would be elicited from the same woman if another woman were asking the same questions. Poll-takers try to avoid risky pairings (such as whites interviewing blacks, or vice versa, on racial issues) if possible.

The snapshot nature of political polls leads to a prime warning of which journalists must be aware: A specific polling result on a specific day or weekend — like Dick Clark's big October lead — usually is less revealing than the *trend* that may be traced from one poll to another.

Imagine a comparison, for instance, in which a respected poll-taker, in successive surveys, finds the candidates running neck and neck. But in his final poll, published the day before the vote, Candidate X is predicted to win by about eight points.

Another poll, by an equally respected opinion researcher, has consistently shown Candidate X well ahead, but by declining margins. In the final pre-election poll of this second researcher, Candidate X still

---

[11] Indeed, it does. Participants in the year 2000 presidential-election debates were limited to those who had averaged 15 percent support in several of these major-media polls taken earlier that year. Never mind that these "snapshots" of the electorate may change as the campaign year goes along. Third-party or independent candidates were shut out of the debates, which meant virtually out of the election.

leads but by a small margin. When the actual votes are counted, Candidate X wins by about eight points.

Which poll was more nearly correct? The one that accurately predicted the winning margin on Election Day, even if that contradicted its campaign-long insistence that the race was close? Or the one that predicted the winner all along, and by declining margins, even though finally predicting a victory for X by a smaller percentage than the voters actually gave him?

In other words, is the final margin of victory more important than a reasonably accurate depiction of the state of the campaign? Most poll-takers and journalists sophisticated about polling would say that "the dynamic" or "the trend" in any election is more instructive than a specific result on a given day.

Suppose Candidate A (to change the example) is ahead of B by 10 points on Sept. 15, which is not such a big lead if the margin of error is plus-or-minus three. But a poll on Oct. 10 shows the race to have fallen within that margin of error. The most important conclusion to be drawn, then, is not just that it's a close election but that in less than a month A has slipped and B has gained.

That change would be significant even if A had dropped from a commanding 20-point lead to only 15. Is the trend likely to continue? What caused it? In either case, A's declining lead should be a signal not only to her to get cracking, and to B to take heart and keep working, but to the poll-taker to continue surveying and to do so perhaps even more often. Above all, the change should be a signal to a journalist covering the campaign to look at it again with a fresh eye. Maybe Candidate B, like Seattle Slew,[12] was counted out too soon. As Tom Dewey and Dick Clark could attest, in politics it ain't necessarily over when the fat lady sings; it ain't over till it's over.

Let me come full circle to that polling booth I entered in 1948, ready to confound my life's history and my father's faith by voting Republican. I was going to take such drastic action at least partly because I had been convinced by poll findings, accepted and trumpeted by the press, that the little man on the wedding cake was bound to win. But in the end, what Lincoln called "the better angels" of my

---

[12] A famous racehorse who consistently ran behind, then came on strong to win in the end.

nature prevailed, and I'll be forever glad to say that I cast my first presidential vote for Harry S Truman.

How many voters, nevertheless, have cast their ballots — as I nearly did — because (a) polls and the press have persuaded them that one candidate or another is going to win, and (b) no one wants to vote for a sure loser?[13] No figures exist, or perhaps ever will, on this effect of the modern American reliance on political polling. The one sure thing is that the effect must exist.

Journalists, therefore, should be careful not to magnify this effect. They should not conclude, for a familiar example, that because the polls say so, a Thomas Dewey or a Dick Clark can't lose, and they should not pass that conclusion on to readers and viewers, who deserve better of a press on which they must rely (however reluctantly). No subject more than polling, and particularly press reliance on polls in political coverage, demands more skepticism — that indispensable quality of the best journalists.

Most polls are honest and useful, are based solidly on statistical knowledge, and tell us a great deal about candidates, parties, issues, government — even ourselves. They're not Holy Writ, however, and journalists must pass them to an expectant public with proper warnings against the occasional fraud, error or oversell.

---

[13] Third-party candidates, like George Wallace in 1968 and John Anderson in 1980, often start out with an impressive poll showing. By Election Day, when it's certain that they're losers, their poll standings are significantly lower. So are their final vote totals.

CHAPTER 10

Control

In October 1996, *Consumer Reports* declared that the Isuzu Trooper, a popular sports utility vehicle (SUV), was unsafe. In April 2000, a jury in Los Angeles found that, in its article and at a news conference, the magazine had made false statements. One of these false statements was that the Trooper had a tendency to tip over when swerving to avoid an object in the road.

Therefore, it may seem strange and contradictory, even indefensible, that Consumers Union, the nonprofit publisher of *Consumer Reports,* actually won the case and avoided damage payments. It could do so because the jury also found that the false statements had not materially damaged Isuzu and, perhaps most important, had not been made maliciously.

In a libel case, if a false statement is found to have been made "with malice," that means — regardless of what the dictionary says — that the accused journal or broadcaster did not even make a good-faith effort to learn whether the statement really was false. The conclusion that *Consumer Reports* had *not* acted maliciously — it had conducted actual driving tests — meant that the jury believed the magazine had honestly believed the statements it made were true. Therefore, under the law as interpreted by the Supreme Court, there could be no libel judgment.

The jury nevertheless found that *Consumer Reports* was incorrect to claim that the Trooper had a "unique and extremely dangerous propensity to roll over in a real-world emergency avoidance maneuver." The National Highway Traffic Safety Administration also had reported that sports utility vehicles like the Trooper have a tendency to roll over, owing to their high center of gravity. But the federal agency attributed the danger not to sudden swerving, as *Consumer Reports* had, but to the SUV being "tripped" by running up on a curb or a smaller vehicle.

Isuzu claimed that the magazine's tests were rigged. The jury rejected that idea but Jonathan Kotler, a professor of media law at the University of Southern California, pointed out that even though the company lost the case, it achieved most of what it "reasonably could have expected" — probable damage to the credibility of the magazine as well as whatever legal costs Consumers Union had had to bear in defending its magazine's statements.

Other analysts saw the suit and the verdict as a standoff in which both sides could claim victory: Isuzu for having won the false-statement verdict, Consumers Union and its magazine for having escaped monetary damages and the charge of malice. As Robert C. Post, a law professor at the University of California, put it, *Consumer Reports* received a "slap on the wrist" but not a "punch in the nose."[1]

The real victor may have been neither side but an important aspect of freedom of the press — the right of a publication or broadcaster to carry negative reviews of a product, whether artistic or commercial. The Los Angeles decision essentially followed an earlier Supreme Court ruling that even a false charge, if made without malice (in the meaning of the word applied to libel cases), might be essential to the "robust and wide-open debate" guaranteed, in effect, to the American people by the First Amendment to the Constitution.

If qualified movie reviewers, for instance, assert that a film is not worth the price of admission, they have not committed a libel because they cannot be shown to have acted with malice even if other, equally qualified persons later award the movie an Oscar. Similarly, if a political commentator for a television station offers an opinion based on the observation that a particular candidate is "running like a dry creek," the commentator is entirely within his or her constitutional rights even if the candidate goes on to win in a landslide.

Or if a respected consumer guardian like *Consumer Reports,* long familiar to its 4.3 million readers, after having made a good-faith effort to ascertain the truth, criticizes a popular commercial product, it may have made a mistake, but it has not committed a libel.

This interpretation of the First Amendment hardly means, however, that the American press has no need to concern itself with libel so long as it makes an honest effort to ascertain the truth of whatever it makes pub-

---

[1] The Kotler and Post comments were reported in *The New York Times,* April 8, 2000, in a story from Los Angeles by Andrew Pollack.

lic. That's why the Isuzu-Consumers Union case was much to the point of whether the American press is as free and as free-wheeling — many believe *too* powerful, *too* independent — as its critics like to charge.

The fact is that, whether or not Isuzu intended to intimidate Consumers Union by suing its magazine, a lawsuit for libel has a so-called chilling effect that *does* intimidate not just the defendant, but the media in general. Professor Kotler put his finger on it: Isuzu's lawsuit in and of itself, no matter what the outcome, threatened and perhaps damaged *Consumer Reports'* credibility, particularly with anyone who already doubted the magazine's honesty or that of the press generally. The suit also must have cost Consumers Union some hefty legal fees. No news agency wants to face such possible consequences, and some literally can't afford the fees.

In the Isuzu case, the suit came after the charges had been published. The true chilling effect of a libel suit, however, is in the *threat* of it, and the effect of such a threat is not limited to the party being sued. Rather, it intimidates less affluent publishers and broadcasters for whom high legal costs might be prohibitive; less-established news agencies whose credibility may be fragile; and the rest of the press, owing to its concern that some day in some case some libel suit may lead to a more threatening interpretation of the law than the one that now prevails.

Who knows how many critical stories about products, persons or companies have not been published or aired, precisely because those who could have made such stories public had to consider the unpleasant consequences of a possible libel suit? Even if they believed the story true and without malice, they legitimately had to worry about (a) the possibility that even an unjustified lawsuit might damage their credibility, and (b) that they might incur the sizable costs of defending against such a suit perhaps all the way to the Supreme Court. No one knows, since no statistics exist about stories *not* published or aired.

It's safe, however, to suppose that no one pondering whether to make public a story that will damage a powerful person or company or institution is likely to do so without considering whether a suit for libel will result (even if there's no doubt the story is true and malice can't be proven). It's also highly likely that in some situations some newspapers or broadcasters have decided not to publicize a controversial story in order to avoid the real risk of being sued.

The other side of that coin is that a company that believes itself about to be maligned may decide strategically to threaten suit, even if the company privately believes that it has little chance to win under present law. As Professor Kotler pointed out, a suit may well damage a news agency's credibility (where there's smoke, there must be fire, some in the public are likely to think); and a court defense certainly will cost the accused publisher or broadcaster a lot of money. Maybe that publisher or broadcaster can be scared off, particularly if the threatening concern already has a litigious reputation, which, in itself, may be sufficient to prevent publication or broadcast.

So if the *fact* of libel is difficult to prove, the *threat* of libel is easy to invoke and may be even more effective. The threat might possibly prevent the publication or broadcast of accusative stories and may at least punish news agencies after the fact. That's why libel remains a real concern for publishers and broadcasters, though the state of American law is more favorable to the press than it ever has been.

Still, libel suits and even the threat of such suits, though potent, are not the major inhibitions on a free press. There are many other inhibitions — some inherent, some self-inflicted.

WHAT "LINE"?

Chapter 8 discusses in detail how competition, though mostly a positive factor in journalism, can cause errors of misunderstanding, panic, omission, commission and outright fraud. Competition often involves catching up to other newspapers or networks or making the effort to get ahead of them — in broadcasting, even by a few seconds. Competition is therefore a useful limitation on the much-exaggerated power of the press.

Much-exaggerated is not synonymous, of course, with *nonexistent*. The press in America is indeed powerful, but Woodrow Wilson properly defined its power when he called the news "the atmosphere of events." Just as people wear overcoats when it's cold and short sleeves when it's hot, and in politics charge begets charge, the atmosphere of events influences virtually everything that happens within it.

The press cannot, however, as too often suggested, propagate anything it pleases, any lie or propaganda, any story true or false. A century ago, the Hearst newspapers could produce the atmosphere in which a war with Spain over Cuba could be popular. Perhaps print media could create such an atmosphere today, just as television may have made it possible for President George Bush to send troops to Somalia in the early 1990s. But the press could not, then or now, declare or actually launch the Spanish-American or any war. It wasn't the press that sent a half-million Americans to fight in Vietnam, though that war might have been possible only in that particular atmosphere of events.

The press is not a monolith, particularly now that radio and television, network and cable, have been added to the print media and now that the Internet is growing swiftly. So many press organs exist, in so many different circumstances — of ownership, community, tradition, politics, technology — that no single view, certainly no contrived version of events, can be foisted off on the public by any one news outlet or any small group of them.

One newspaper checks another; one television station balances a second. A false or misleading story will be ignored or corrected or even denounced in other publications or broadcasts, much as the checks and balances built into the Constitution prevent any of the three branches of government from dominating the others.

Even if, in the hustle of competition, one or more newspapers pick up and reprint a questionable story from its originator, the contamination will not inexorably spread, as would a computer virus, throughout the press. Some news organization somewhere will check, refute or challenge it. The diversity of the press — not just print and broadcasting but the hundreds of individual news agencies within each — means that neither false information nor biased advocacy nor any particular "line" is likely to go unchallenged and that false stories will be refuted if necessary. (But see "The Club" section below.)

Any fair-minded study discloses that the American press is many-faceted. It is not composed, for instance, of all Republican or all Democratic organs. It's not all tabloid or *The New York Times,* all History Channel or Entertainment Tonight. It's not all metropolitan and not all rural or small town; some editorial pages are interested in foreign affairs and some are anything but. And the press is certainly not all liberal.

Harry Truman used to denounce "the Republican press," but the headlines in that press favored and facilitated his reelection in 1948. Probably the most identifiably ideological newspaper in the United States is the staunchly conservative Republican — and proud of it — *Union Leader* of Manchester, N.H. Since "the world's greatest newspaper," as the conservative *Chicago Tribune* calls itself, now owns the *Los Angeles Times,* once the Republican arbiter of California politics, it dominates two of the three largest markets in the country. On the airwaves, the most listened to and talked of commentator is Rush Limbaugh, who never met a liberal cause he couldn't denounce.

The variety of the press — talk radio to the contrary — acts as a check and balance within what's been called "the fourth branch of government." This variety also virtually precludes the popular notion of a "liberal press conspiracy." That silly idea presupposes the impossible, that the owners and operators of the major news outlets get together periodically and decide on what Richard Nixon used to call "the line," an overall message that the press — like stampeding cattle — will then dutifully follow.

Not only are those owners and operators business competitors, but they are diverse human beings, as different as Ted Turner and Katharine Graham. They may all be devoted, it's true, to making a profit, but they are not all in pursuit of the same political or govern-mental theory. Nor are they all dedicated to any one person's election or to any particular interest. The idea that such a group could agree on *anything* unanimously, or even by, say, 60 to 40, and then could impose that view on the press as a whole, and that the rest of the press would be subservient enough to follow the agreed-upon "line" — such a fantasy, when analyzed, falls of its own weight. Without a Stalin or a Hitler in Washington to dictate it, there is and can be no press "line," except as the product of critics' fear and paranoia.

So if diversity and competition act as both an internal auditor and a barrier to conspiracy, real limitations on the imagined power of the press exist within the press itself. These limitations greatly diminish that menace too many Americans imagine looming over them like the dark and twisting plume of a tornado.

THE CLUB

As noted, however, the owners and operators of the press are all devoted to making a profit. That's not so much a conspiracy as a com-munity of interest or a natural tendency, not unlike the impulse to eat, drink and survive. No publisher or broadcast executive has to conspire with another to pursue the mutual goal of profit. After all, they do have to meet a payroll, fulfill contracts and produce next week's and next year's publication and broadcasts. They have to stay in business.

All members of this Club — which has no constitution or bylaws and needs none — are necessarily committed to capitalism, free enter-prise and profit, although there may be minor variations in their philosophies. One, for example, may support the minimum wage, another may regard it as communistic; a few mavericks may even favor a stiff capital-gains tax.

The main point is clear in their minds, however, though few members of the Club fill their columns or airwaves with obvious capitalist propaganda. All of them share the basic Club view that industry, business, investment, trade and profit (especially their own) are to be prized and encouraged, sometimes to the detriment of such other values as environmental protection or employee welfare. All are part of free enterprise and believe free enterprise can only flourish in a free society like America's, where anyone can and everyone should pursue the American dream of making money.

If there were such a thing, the Club view would come close to being the established American philosophy. Because that Club view is so widespread — so conventional — any contrary or more than mildly dissenting approach is seldom to be read or heard in the American press. Again, that's not because of a press conspiracy to suppress certain ideas. Instead it's because of the herd instinct of the Establishment, of which the Club is a fully functioning subcommittee. Indeed, the belief in free enterprise and making money is the nearest thing to a "line" followed by the American press.

Newspapers, magazines and radio and television stations, after all, are *businesses*. In the broadcast media, and more and more often in print, news and journalism take a distinct second place to entertainment. These businesses often are highly profitable, sometimes ranking among the biggest enterprises in a community. Those who own or operate such businesses are not likely to be anything but enthusiastic supporters of the free enterprise that has made them so often rich and powerful.

Those outside journalism who share the Club's conventional economic doctrine may not consider it a limitation on the power of the press. Indeed, nonjournalists often feel that Club members are too timid or too reluctant (or, for some inexplicable reason, too un-American) to assert that doctrine forcefully. Many even go a step further: They believe that the press is not just too liberal or left-leaning but possibly even socialist or communist (though rarely is a distinction made between these terms).

Those who dissent from the Club attitude, on the other hand, are likely to believe that the American press is limited in its perceptions of the world around it. They believe, for instance, that poverty, slums, crime, race distinctions and the lack of health care are reported in the press, if at all, less with understanding or sympathy than with criticism and an eye to exploitation. From this attitude, the conviction that the press is controlled by big bosses, big business, big advertisers and big money is an easy extrapolation.

Those who hold either of these conflicting views of the press, which apparently is quite a few Americans, tend not to believe what they see or read.

Another way in which Club attitudes reduce the power of the press is the fact that few Club members can face the loss of profit. (Who can?) Shrinking advertising or circulation revenues often result in the closing or consolidation of valuable news agencies, leaving the press with fewer voices and less diversity. On the other hand, the siren lure of profit may cause Club members to replace, or at least give them reason to replace, unprofitable journalistic values, such as serving the public interest, with financial or ideological values, such as serving private interests. When Disney buys the American Broadcasting Company, including ABC News, or when the Rev. Sun Myung Moon takes over United Press International, the actions were not taken in order to pursue "robust and wide-open" debate.

Members of the Club, moreover, don't resign, as journalist Helen Thomas of UPI did to protest the Moonie purchase. Rather, they sell out.

BLOWING WINDS

Imagine the following: A hurricane destroys thousands of buildings and acres of land in Central America. Before the story can be fully told, an earthquake levels whole communities in Turkey. And just as the world's press begins to focus on the quake, epic floods wash over a devastated countryside in Mozambique.

That's what I call "dailiness" and what James Reston used to describe with a telling phrase: "Christ, how the wind blew!"

In other words, waves of news from around the world can drench newsrooms everywhere in fresh catastrophe, additional agony and more death and destruction, even sometimes as good news continues to flood in simultaneously. And though the natural disasters I cited may not literally happen in one weekend, or over a few days, journalism often is awash in continually breaking news, different stories from different places at once, the world seemingly erupting.

Sometimes Reston's blowing wind so overwhelms any single event or series of happenings that all the news can't be completely or adequately reported in any newspaper or broadcast. Nor is the tide of dailiness limited to nature's convulsions, as can be seen by a glance at any American newspaper on the second Wednesday after the first Monday of every fourth year.

That's the day when these newspapers report what happened on Tuesday, national Election Day, when occupants of virtually every office of significance throughout the land are elected. It may well be that to the voters of a particular city in the Midwest their mayoralty race was the most important of the day, but neither *The New York Times* nor *The Washington Post* will have much of a story about it. The two big Eastern newspapers were preoccupied with the presidential election, gubernatorial and other races in their circulation areas, learned disquisitions by their political writers.

In the first chapter of this book, I noted that on election night of 1960 — when returns in the exciting Kennedy-Nixon presidential election were coming into the *Times* newsroom — I was assigned to write one story about all of the important gubernatorial races in the nation. I don't remember how many governors' races there were, or how important nationally, but I do recall that my story was less than a column in length and that I finished writing it in plenty of time to observe my colleagues concentrating on the presidential election. Dailiness caused the *Times,* which then still prided itself on being "the newspaper of record," to focus on what was *nationally* important while dozens of newspapers and broadcasters necessarily zeroed in on *local* returns.

Another aspect of dailiness is the never-ending flow of news to agencies that try to cover the world: millions of words a day pouring off the clacking tickers. Events of consequence seem to follow one another as inevitably as the night the day. Before one can be handled well, another is clamoring for attention on the wires or the satellites. The predictable results are that important events too often get too little space in the paper or time on the air, and too little comprehension or knowledge gets into the reporting of the story. And then it's on to the next hurried report, the next perhaps misleading story or headline, the next haste-plagued edition.

For a number of reasons, *The New York Times* no longer claims to be *the* or even scarcely *a* newspaper of record. Communications have advanced in ease, speed, reach and comprehensiveness (and continue to advance on the World Wide Web); television has put most important events on film or tape and on satellites for worldwide transmission; more nations demand journalists' attention; science and the arts gain in interest and relevance. As a result, the sheer volume of "the record" has become impossible to report in its entirety.

No newspaper and no broadcaster can any longer provide a complete account of events. Now, for something like such an account, a studious person would have to read several daily newspapers (American and foreign), one or more weekly newsmagazines and perhaps a monthly, stay tuned to the Cable News Network, switch often to one of the over-the-air networks, listen to the most important radio reports (even when driving) and command quick access to the Internet.

Even for those who could maintain such a regimen, it might still be necessary to keep up with books published or documentary films shown long after an event. With more time available and more sources willing and able to talk, these books or films might overcome dailiness sufficiently to present a comprehensive inside account of what really happened, for what reasons and with what consequences. That's hard to do for journalists trying to deal immediately with events.

I have been surprised and somewhat saddened by reading Frances Fitzgerald's account of the Reagan administration and Rick Perlstein's book about the rise of Barry Goldwater and organized conservatism in the 1950s and 1960s.[2] These detailed retrospectives told me a great deal that, unhappily, I didn't know at the time, though I was an active journalist during the careers of Goldwater and Reagan. Hindsight and research, of course, can fill in many blanks in what any contemporary journalist is likely to know.

So, as history becomes more complex and more swiftly accessible in more forms to more people in more places, and as virtual simulations of what once was considered reality become more accepted, conventional newspapers and broadcasters are finding it more difficult to perform journalism's traditional task. Journalists have always tried to "catch history on the wing" as well as to understand and explain it. But today, relentless, insidious — how the wind blows! — dailiness inhibits the ability of the press to serve, much less dominate (as popularly supposed), the public's understanding.

THE TWO MORGUES

The vast library of clippings from their own issues kept by most publications (now preserved mainly on microfilm or microfiche) is traditionally known as "the morgue," a vital resource for any purveyor of news. If writing about the economic summit of 2000, a reporter can go

---

[2] Frances Fitzgerald, *Way Out There in the Blue* (New York: Simon & Schuster, 2000); Rick Perlstein, *Before the Storm: Barry Goldwater and the Unmaking of the American Consensus* (New York: Hill and Wang, 2001).

to the morgue and do research on what happened at the summits of 1999 or 1985 or on any other event that might affect the story. A news morgue actually is pretty close to a "first draft of history" — though, like all drafts, in need of editing, supplementing and updating.

What about all those off-the-record, background and deep background statements journalists consented to hear but not to report completely? Only what was printed or broadcast is in the morgue. What about classified documents to which journalists, but not the public, have been permitted limited access? What about the informed gossip that circulates in every newsroom, print or broadcast, but can't be publicized because the source insists on anonymity or was speaking privately? And what about all those informal conversations journalists may have had over the lunch table or the martini glass with important sources?

What, in short, about all the information journalists know but never commit to print or film because they can't or won't?

Alas! All that kind of information — and it's usually a lot — goes to a quite different kind of morgue. It's buried in the minds and memories of individual journalists and may never be communicated to anyone, save perhaps a wife or a husband or a memoir to be written far in the future. One of the "dirty little secrets" of the news business, therefore — and a profound limitation on the power of the press — is that journalists always know, or think they know, more than they can or will tell the public they're supposed to serve.

NOTHING'S HAPPENING

In Chapter 2, I noted that news can be something that *didn't* happen — no crimes in the city yesterday; Barry Bonds didn't hit a home run — if that something had been expected to happen or might conceivably have happened. The absence of an anticipated event, then, can be an event in itself. Colin Powell, for instance, got headlines because he did *not* run for president in 1996.

What if, however, an event takes place where nothing is believed or expected to be happening? According to the usual press practice, that's probably not news, as in the familiar conundrum of the tree falling in the forest with no one to hear. Was there a crash? Similarly, does an unrecorded event actually happen?

News organizations generally believe, for example, that "nothing's happening" in a prison unless there's (a) a riot, (b) an escape, preferably multiple, or (c) the murder of a corrections officer. But prisons are only *believed* to be subdued places where nothing's happening. In fact, on any day, in any state or federal prison, there may routinely be violence, drug dealing and consequent crime, administrative mishap or chicanery, perhaps rape, and frequent miscarriages of justice.

Events of that kind usually make the news, in print and on the air — but not if they occur in a prison because journalists believe nothing's happening behind those reassuring walls. And where journalists believe nothing's happening, often nothing does happen as far as notice in the press is concerned.

The result is another gaping hole in the feared omnipotence of the press. For every loudly denounced press invasion of someone's privacy, actual or imagined, there may also be an unnoticed, unreported story of human passion, folly, nobility or cussedness. Events of institutional interest may also go unnoticed, such as the executives of a corporation deciding to dump toxics in a convenient stream.

Journalism, too often believing "nothing's happening," fails to pay everyday attention not only to prisons but to businesses large and small, to routine bureaucracies, the public schools[3] (not school boards or teachers' unions), hospitals (save for administrative foul-ups or malpractice scandals), all sorts of historical and artistic institutions, thousands of both lower and higher courtrooms, innumerable congressional committee meetings and hearings, and their local and state counterparts.

Even in the military, except for combat zones and the more prominent Pentagon and command levels, nothing worth reporting is usually believed to be happening. For many years, the press itself — before it became controversial as "the media" — could have been added to that list. Now, like an anxious blood-pressure patient, the press constantly examines itself with alarm.

When, however, was the last time you read a story about the internal administrative decisions of a major corporation's board of directors? When did you last see a story about night-court proceedings in a major city? How do you or how does anyone keep up with the rulings of the Federal Trade Commission? Or your state Department of Motor Vehicles? Or your local city purchasing office?

The press doesn't even provide sustained coverage of the thousands of sometimes routine but often important cases heard in the fed-

---

[3] Recent events like the massacre at Columbine High School in Colorado may have brought schools themselves under closer watch.

eral appeals courts, which are only one step below the Supreme Court.[4]
No journalist should be comfortable with the view of Judge Gilbert
Merritt of the 6th Circuit Court of Appeals:

> At the court of appeals level we're neither fish nor fowl. We're not
> local, and we're not national . . . we couldn't get the press interested
> because they're not interested in the processes of the court.[5]

These huge uncovered areas, among many others, can largely be
explained by the sheer magnitude of the job of reporting the news.
Despite its boasts, the press can't cover everything. If it tried to, no
newspaper could afford the paper and no broadcaster the ad-free time,
and neither could afford the staff. Too much is happening, or might happen, in the city, the state, the nation, the world and even the universe.

Choices have to be made, and experience usually defines the public's greater interests. Thus the press tends to focus on war, violence,
sex, crime, race, celebrities, sports, politics and the economy. Seldom
does it zero in on the routine activities of administration, bureaucracy,
education, courts and the military. Nor do journalists cover other institutions unless they become involved in controversy (as when the
Brooklyn Museum of Art was savaged by New York's Mayor Rudolph
Giuliani for staging a supposedly sacrilegious exhibition) or low-level
legislative committee meetings, where, unfortunately, the real work of
serving or exploiting the public often is done.

Committees of Congress used to pursue the ancient custom of
holding their most important sessions behind closed doors. In those bad
old days, the elderly but enterprising reporter for the *Times* Washington
bureau, C. P. "Peck" Trussell, sometimes used an old-fashioned hearing
aid to thwart this arrogant secrecy. The aid was attached to a prominent
microphone on his chest. Peck would hold this mike against the committee's closed door, take notes on what he heard and then return to the
office with a useful exclusive.

Unfortunately, the press doesn't often have a microphone (at least
not legally) that can penetrate even into places where "nothing's
happening." And the sheer volume of the world's recognizable news,
forcing the press to make hard choices about what and how much it

---

[4] In 1997, 52,315 cases were filed in federal appeals courts. The Supreme Court
reviews perhaps a hundred of these cases annually.
[5] Wallace Westfeldt and Tom Wicker, *Indictment* (Nashville: The First Amendment
Center), p. 5.

can cover, leaves much human, often important (or at least dramatic) activity to fall between the cracks of the beats that virtually every news agency relies on.

(Maybe they shouldn't rely on such beats. One of the best jobs of covering Washington was done in the last days of the *New York Herald-Tribune*. For reasons of economy, the *H-T*'s Washington bureau staff had been cut to a handful of reporters. The bureau's resourceful chief, David Wise, did away with beats and deployed his troops to find what news they could, as best they could, anywhere they could. They found a lot of it and regularly gave the conventional *Times* beat reporters fits.)

It is all very well to have a watchful reporter at the Pentagon, the governor's office, the city council or the school board meeting on the White House beat. These are obvious places to cover. But it should be just as obvious that if no one is assigned to cover school classrooms or playgrounds, apparently peaceful prisons, museums, routine military exercises or overcrowded courts (where an overworked judge hears and disposes of dozens of "minor" cases in a morning), nothing that goes on in such venues will make news, even on the back pages.

CHURCH AND STATE

Not merely because of his handy hearing aid, Peck Trussell was the grand old man of the *Times* Washington bureau when I worked there. The question once arose whether a straight-news reporter might ethically write an editorial on a subject in his field of expertise. Scotty Reston, opposing the notion, asked Peck what had been the policy on the *Sun*.

Without a moment's hesitation, he replied: "Absolute separation of church and state!" That was the end of *that* discussion.

What's even more important, however, is that "absolute separation" should be maintained between *advertising* and the news. *The New York Times* gained much of its eminence when World War II caused newsprint to be rationed; most newspapers cut back on the space devoted to news while keeping their advertising sections intact. The *Times* reduced its advertising columns instead and kept printing all the news from the war fronts.

Even today, it's the editor's prerogative to throw ads out of the *Times* if extra space is needed for one or more major stories. When advertisers in a chain of medical journals owned by the *Times* brought certain pressures, the *Times* sold the chain rather than yield. Elsewhere in journalism, though, church and state are not always so thoroughly walled off from each other.

The *Los Angeles Times* openly experimented in recent years with breaking down the wall between advertising and the news. The effort led to a virtual staff revolt and to the downfall of the publisher. When Bill Kovach, one of the journalists other journalists most respect, became editor of the Cox Newspapers in Atlanta, he not only shook them up by winning two Pulitzers in two years but also shook up that city, which is not an easy thing to do. His brand of watchdog journalism so alarmed the city's power structure, as well as specific advertisers, that many of Atlanta's leaders protested to Cox headquarters. Kovach was ordered to tone things down.

He resigned rather than comply. Atlanta's loss became journalism's gain when Kovach then was appointed curator of the Nieman Foundation at Harvard, where he would work with promising journalists from around the world.

Certain dismaying signs suggest that as the Internet becomes more important, the line — it's not always a wall — between advertising and news may be often blurred, if not broken. The merger of Time Warner and America Online was hailed primarily as creating a vast new medium for shopping, entertainment and interpersonal communication; the journalism of *Time* Magazine and the Cable News Network (now an element of Time Warner) was scarcely mentioned and seems not to be a high priority for the gigantic new company.

Aside from these threatening developments, some publications and broadcasters too nearly emulate the attitude candidly expressed by Lord Thomson of Fleet, when he was a chain newspaper publisher in Europe and North America:

> I buy newspapers to make money to buy more newspapers to make more money. As for editorial content, that's the stuff you separate the ads with.

Members of the Club are not usually that frank, but Lord Thomson's view may express something like the private attitude many hold. Still, it's a rare event when even a major advertiser can *demand* that a news organization do or not do something in which the advertiser is interested. Most publishers are not that easy to push around; many, probably including Lord Thomson in his heyday, have at least a public-relations fear of appearing to be dominated by advertisers; and the advertiser often needs to advertise more than a newspaper or broadcaster needs to sell space or time. It's a demonstrable fact that other advertisers usually will clamor to replace one who withdraws an ad. Some media, facing heavy demand for their space or time, actually have to reject ads, which is what happens to the TV network that is broadcasting the Super Bowl in any given year.

The most effective advertising pressures, moreover, are those that publishers and broadcasters bring on themselves, in fear that some story or program will offend a potential or actual advertiser. If advance word gets out that, say, a broadcast might be offensive to "family values," perhaps an advertiser will withdraw scheduled ads or not buy space or time in the future. Such an implicit threat, even if never expressed in words or deeds, is not dissimilar to the chilling effect of a potential libel suit. Rather than run the risk of such advertiser displeasure, the publisher or broadcaster may take counsel of fear and decide not to carry the potentially offensive article or broadcast.

Not just money may be at stake (though money always is). If an advertiser pulls an ad and makes a public denunciation of a publication or a broadcast because it contains, say, too much sex or violence, some segments of the public may react not against the irate advertiser but against the accused publisher or broadcaster. That can happen even if the charge is overstated and the supposedly offensive material turns out to be quite acceptable. As journalists should know, the defense seldom quite catches up to the charge.

Here again, as with potential libel suits, no statistics are available to tell us how many news or feature stories have not been printed or aired in fear of advertiser reaction. There may well have been a lot and there may be more in the future — another way in which the supposed power of the press is not quite as awesome as its critics would have the public believe.

THAT OUGHT NOT TO BE ALLOWED

In September 1997, the class I was teaching at Davidson College discussed the accidental death of Princess Diana, which was then thought to have been caused in part by paparazzi pursuing her speeding car. An irate student suggested that photographers "ought not to be allowed" to take pictures of people without their consent. But suppose, I replied, the photographer is using a long-range lens to get a shot of the mayor having lunch with a known mafioso.

The class went back and forth on that question and never reached a final consensus, but the student's comment seemed to me to be typical. Time and again, people will say that something in the press "ought not to be allowed": stakeouts at private houses, ambush interviews on television or journalists posing as supermarket workers. Many people believe that any number of activities by which someone in the press offends someone in the public just "ought not to be allowed."

By whom?

That's a question few critics seem to have considered. What they're protesting may indeed be in bad taste or constitute bad journalism (such as unnecessary reliance on anonymous sources). But if the activity "ought not to be allowed," doesn't that presuppose that someone has the power and authority to forbid it and then to enforce such a ruling?

Who?

Obviously, only one entity has both the power and the reach to impose its will on the myriad organs of the American press: newspapers — large and small, daily and weekly, commercial and "alternative," school and church — radio at home and in autos and bars, spectrum and cable television, movie theaters, video shops, magazines, desktop publishers, the Internet and all its offspring, zealots with a mimeograph machine in the basement, and on and on.

Only one entity could possibly say to all those elements of the press, "that's not allowed," and make it stick — much less, "you must" do so-and-so. That entity is, of course, the federal government, which has the reach and, if it wanted to use it, perhaps the power.

Hitler had both the reach and the power, and so did Stalin. But unlike them, the U.S. government doesn't have the authority. Congress, the legislative branch that would have to pass the necessary laws, can't even find a constitutional means of keeping pornography off the Internet. Apparently, there isn't any, because the First Amendment stands in the way:

> Congress shall make no law . . . abridging the freedom of speech or of the press . . .

So even if everyone could agree that something the press does "ought not to be allowed," no one and nothing in the United States has the necessary authority successfully to forbid that something. The First Amendment would have to be repealed. And that could only happen through a vote of the people's representatives, who'd have to pass another amendment repealing the First, or at least its passage shielding the press. Such an amendment would require the approval of two-thirds of the members of each house of Congress and three-fourths of the states.

Some polls suggest that in a national referendum — a different, less-binding procedure than amending the Constitution — the American people might opt to do away with freedom of the press. Maybe they would. In 1991, in a commencement address at Samford College in Birmingham, Ala., I discussed government control of information during the then-recent Gulf War. The audience applauded — not for my denunciation but for government control!

I'd like to believe that the applause was more a celebration of the "smart" missiles cleverly allowed to be featured on wartime television than of government manipulation of the news. Depending, however, on the atmosphere of events in which a referendum was held, so unpopular is the press that its freedom might well be voted down. Such a vote, however, would only be what in politics is known as "a beauty contest." It would be no more binding on anybody than a poll.

No referendum or political party or government official or four-star general or celebrity — not even a president — can abolish freedom of the press in America. Only the demanding process of constitutional amendment could do that. And even if that were to happen, some "power" still would have to act as censor, to enforce what would no longer be allowed. Again, only one power could do it.

The truth that critics seldom face is the choice implicit in the cry that something "ought not to be allowed." There are two realistic options before the American people: (a) government control and probable government manipulation of news reporting or (b) the sometimes chaotic, sometimes pernicious, often beneficial diversity of a free press.

If Americans faced up to that choice — decisively rather than in a beauty contest — it's unlikely they'd choose government control. Since they stoutly resist any suggestion that Washington should take charge of business or religion or medicine or sports, why should they want it to command the press? Freedom from government control, though sometimes breached, is the American tradition, the American pride.

Americans do, however, want the press to be responsible. And who could dispute that goal? Journalists certainly would not; they think of themselves as serving the public. The difficulty is that there's never a single, inarguable answer to perhaps the most crucial question in journalism: What, in any disputed situation, *is* responsible behavior? You may not admire some press practices, and I may deplore others. But many of our fellow citizens would approve the very things we oppose — or rail against what's actually done.

So again, we are faced with a fundamental choice:

Who do you want to decide what's responsible reporting of the news and what's not? An inevitably self-serving government? Or a diversified, competitive, checked and balanced free press, committed to (though sometimes ducking) the quest for truth?

For me, and I hope for most Americans, the choice is not hard. The question answers itself.

Index

ABC News, 3
Advertising, separation between news
   and, 150–52
Alsop brothers, 124
Ambush interviews, 101–2
America Online, Time-Warner
   merger with, 151
American Broadcasting Company,
   144
Anderson, John, 136n
Angelette, Michael, 44
Anonymity provided to speaker, 63,
   70, 72
Attribution to source, 62, 71, 73

Backgrounder, 26, 54, 62–63, 65–68,
   73–74, 75, 147
   deep, 74–75, 147
Bacon, Worth, 87, 98
Baker, James, 22
Baker, Russell, 92
Balanced judgment, 72
Bancroft, Harding, 11, 12
Bay of Pigs invasion, 4–7, 12, 41
Beat coverage, 119–20
Bell, Jack, 23
Bender, Jay, 33n
Bernstein, Carl, viii, 61n, 98–99,
   100
Bias, 83
Bland, David, 41–42
Bly, Nellie, 102
Bonds, Barry, 15, 93, 147
Bradlee, Ben, 16, 24, 116
Bradley, Bill, 21, 125
Breaking news, 22–24, 29
Brill, Steven, 73
Brinkley, David, 3

Broadcast news
   contrasts between newspapers and,
   29–30
   See also Television news
Brokaw, Tom, viii, 75
Brooklyn Museum of Art, 149
Brown, Edmund G. "Pat," 79
Brownell, Herbert, 11
Brown v. *Board of Education,* 98
Bunker, Ellsworth, 8–9
Bush, George, in 1992 election, 45,
   46, 86, 126
   sending of troops to Somalia by,
   140
Bush, George W., in 2000 election,
   21–22, 83, 125–26

Call-back stories, 107–8
Camera, use of hidden, 101–2
Carroll, Wallace, 79, 119
Carson, Rachel, 18–19
Carter, Jimmy, 86, 87
   in 1976 election, 86
   in 1980 election, 29
Catledge, Turner, 1, 2, 4, 5, 6–7, 41
Censorship, nonpublication of name
   of rape victim as, 19
Chancellor, John, 28, 79
Chandler, Liz, 34
Childs, Marquis, 124
Choices, need for, in journalism,
   vii–viii, 1–14, 149
Christian, George, 90
Christopher, Warren, 22
Churchill, Winston, 84
CIA, journalistic reverence for, 5
Civil disobedience, 57
Civil rights movement, 18

Off-the-record knowledge, 76
  ambiguity of, 77–78
Op-Ed page, 27, 28
Operation Olympic, 55
Oswald, Lee Harvey, 95
Overholser, Geneva, 16n
Over-nighters, 113–14

Packwood, Robert, 47
Paley, William S., 19
Pearson, Drew, 124
Pentagon Papers, publication of
  in *The New York Times,* 7–12, 14,
    59–60
  in *The Washington Post,* 16
Perlstein, Rick, 146
Perot, H. Ross, 19
Perry, Jim, 130
Photographs, doctoring of, 98
Plagiarism, 111
Polls
  anomalies in, 125
  as basis for political coverage,
    125–27
  cardinal rule of reporting on,
    130–31
  error in, 132
  exit, 125, 131
  flaws in methodology, 123–25
  fundraising and standings in, 127
  margin of error in, 128–29, 135
  nonrespondents as problem in,
    133–34
  random-dialing, 132–33
  sampling in, 128–29, 132–33
  scientific, 123–24
  snapshot nature of, 124, 134–35
  socially responsible reply in, 134
  straw, 123
  weighting in, 131
  wording of questions in, 129–31
Pope, Tommy, 35, 42, 43n
Post, Robert C., 138
Powell, Colin, 19, 39, 147
Powers, Francis Gary, release of,
    23–24
Presidential lying, 96–97

Press, restrictions on, 152–55
Price, Leslie, 42–44
Prior restraint, 59
Privacy rights
  for public figures, 39–40, 44–45
  for sexual assault victims, 19–20,
    33, 35–38, 44–45
  supposed violations of, 47
Public figure, privacy rights of,
    39–40, 44–45
Public interests, journalistic decisions
    about, 52
Public's right to know, 54–59, 62, 66,
    76

Rape victim. *See* Sexual assault
Ravenel, Charles "Pug," 130
Reagan, Ronald, 46–47, 146
  in election of 1980, 29
Reform Party, 18–19
Release date for information, 61–62
Reporters
  generalist versus specialist,
    116–21
  relationship between sources and,
    75–76
  views of, 88–89
  wire service, 22–23
Reporting
  background, experience, and
    instinct in, 92–93, 95–97
  investigative, 98–104
  responsibility in, 154–55
Republican press, 141
Responsible judgment, as factor in
    news coverage, 7
Responsible reporting of the news,
    154–55
Reston, James, v–vi, 5, 7, 10, 12, 17,
    79, 116, 118–19, 144, 150
Rewrite editors, 24
Roosevelt, Franklin D., 79, 127
  in 1936 election, 123
Roosevelt, Theodore, 39
Rosenthal, Abe, 7, 48
Rowan, Carl, 54
Ruby, Jack, 95

Salant, Richard, 16
Salinger, Pierre, 23, 61–62, 65–66
Sampling error, 128–29
Sawyer, Diane, 100–102
Scientific polls, 123–24
Scott, W. Kerr, 123*n*
Seattle Slew, 135
Second-day angle, 113–14
Seigenthaler, John, 103
Sevareid, Eric, 28
Sexual assault, policy of not naming
    victim of, 19–20, 33, 35–38
Sheehan, Neil, 8, 9–10
Shepherd, Sam, 47
Shinn, George, 31–46
Shinn, Jerry, 40, 41
Slanted news, 80, 82, 89–90
Smith, Merriman, 23
Smith, Susan, 35
Smith, William Kennedy, 19–20
Soft news, 26–27, 29, 62
Sosa, Sammy, 15
Sources
    attribution to, 62, 71, 73
    identification of, for classified
        information, 49–50, 53
    need for reliable identified for clas-
        sified information, 68
    need for two unidentified, 68–69
    reasons for using unidentified,
        70–73
    relationship between reporters and,
        75–76
    trustworthiness of, 70–71
Sourcing, 67–68
Spanish-American War, 16, 140
Speaker
    anonymity provided to, 63, 70, 72
Specialist reporters, 116–21
Sperling, Godfrey, 71
Spin, 22
Stabley, Susan, 36
Stalin, 142, 153
Starr, Kenneth, vii
Stolen secrets, publication of, 12
Story matching, 107, 112
Straw polls, 123

Sulzberger, Arthur O., 7, 10, 11, 12,
    14, 29
Sulzberger, Arthur, 16
Sutherland, Frank, 103, 103*n*
Szulc, Tad, 4–5, 6–7

Tagliabue, Paul, 19
Talese, Gay, 4*n*
Talk radio, 141–42
Tega Cay, S.C. case, 31–46
Television news
    competition with newspapers, 3–4,
        115–16
    growth and maturation of, 3
    impact and reach of, 47
    Kennedy's recognition of potential
        of, 3–4
    newspaper reliance on, 2
Ten Commandments, 13–14, 51–52
Thomas, Helen, 144
Thomson, Lord, 151
Thurmond, Strom, 124, 130
Time Warner, merger with America
    Online, 151
Timing, as determining factor, 5–6,
    49, 50–51
Truman, Harry S, 79, 122–25, 136,
    141
Trussell, C. P. "Peck," 25, 149, 150
Truth
    determining, vii
    responsibility for reporting, 40–41
Turner, Ted, 16, 142
Turner, Wallace, 100

Underground reporting. *See* Inves-
    tigative reporting

Value judgment, 68, 70
Van DeMark, Brian, 96*n*
Victim, privacy rights of, 19–20, 33,
    35–38, 44–46
Vietnam War
    exaggeration of American suc-
        cesses in, 8
    My Lai massacre in, 100
    shift in public interest in, 7–8

164   INDEX